Turns out,
I'm fine

Turns out, I'm fine

Judith Lucy

SCRIBNER

SCRIBNER

First published in Australia in 2021 by Scribner, an imprint of Simon & Schuster Australia
Suite 19A, Level 1, Building C, 450 Miller Street, Cammeray, NSW 2062

Sydney New York London Toronto New Delhi
Visit our website at www.simonandschuster.com.au

SCRIBNER and design are registered trademarks of The Gale Group, Inc., used under licence by Simon & Schuster Inc.

10 9 8 7 6 5 4 3 2 1

© Judith Lucy 2021

All rights reserved. No part of this publication may be reproduced, stored in a retrieval system, or transmitted in any form or by any means, electronic, mechanical, photocopying, recording or otherwise, without prior permission of the publisher.

A Cataloguing-in-Publication entry for this book is available from the National Library of Australia
9781760859206 (paperback)
9781760859213 (ebook)

Cover design by Barney Sullivan
Typeset by Midland Typesetters in 12/18.66 pt Sabon
Printed and bound in Australia by Griffin Press

MIX
Paper from responsible sources
FSC® C009448

The paper in this book is FSC® certified. FSC® promotes environmentally responsible, socially beneficial and economically viable management of the world's forests.

For my mothers Jan and Ann

CONTENTS

Introduction   1

Part One: How the Fuck Did I Get Here?   9
1. Can I Blame My Parents for Everything?   11
2. Actually, He Was Quite Heavy: Unpacking My Big Brother   31
3. When I Grow Up, I'll Be a Feminist Princess: School, University and, Uh-Oh, Boys   47
4. Buggerlugs: My Disastrous History with Men   67
5. Genius: Comedy is My Life   95

Part Two: Having the Rug Pulled Out from Under Me   115
6. The Fairytale   117
7. Short-changed: Falling Apart Physically   143
8. Is it a Duck? More Falling Apart   159

Part Three: Trying   **175**
9. One Hot Cunt: Sorting the Body Stuff Out   177
10. How Not to be an Arsehole Person   203
11. Wouldn't be Dead for Quids: The Answer!   223
12. There is No Answer   241

Acknowledgements   255
About the Author   259

Introduction

Towards the end of 2020, an old friend and I went for a walk and reflected on what a motherfucker of a year it had been. Then he turned to me and said, 'You seem to be doing really well, though. In fact, you seem tickety-boo.' I replied, 'Well, I'm fifty-two, it's about time.'

It had certainly taken a while to get to this point, as the years leading up to it had involved the death of my brother, Niall; the worst break-up I'd ever had, which led to a complete existential meltdown; the onset of menopause; a career slump; a financial disaster; and, just to keep things interesting, trying to find my birth father. On top of all that, I'd had a number of revelations about how I'd been living my life and they weren't good. But I'm good now and that's what this book is about: how I got here. It's about coming out the other side of grief, anger and confusion while retaining most of my marbles.

I didn't know for quite a while that *Turns Out, I'm Fine* was going to be about me turning out to be fine because I was too consumed with the inciting incident. This is the term screenwriters use for the event that sets the story in motion. You certainly notice when there isn't one, as I did when I sat through the 1974 Jack Thompson vehicle *Petersen* recently. The writer, David Williamson, just didn't seem that fussed about a plot or tension, although we did see a great deal of a young Jackie Weaver's bush. The incident is usually something pretty dramatic, like a death or a secret being suddenly exposed. In my case, it was a particularly awful end to a relationship.

I didn't know it was a watershed moment at the time. Don't get me wrong, it was the very worst bust-up I'd ever had, and I've had some doozies! (Such as the guy who said he'd left his wife for me and hadn't. Although, with my practical hat on, that really did save everyone a lot of time and effort. No one likes moving, do they?)

Time certainly didn't fly after that watershed break-up, it limped along, making it clear that things were going to get worse before they got better. Not long after it happened a friend said, 'Jude, you haven't even sorted this into the six or seven piles of shit that this is.' My therapist, Glenda, helpfully added, 'Oh Judith, you haven't even smelt the shit yet.' That was exactly how I felt at that moment: there was a long road ahead and as I walked it, the smell of shit was only going to get stronger.

INTRODUCTION

Six months after the split (as in, can I make like a banana and leave the planet?), when I was obviously completely over it and considering getting an audition tape together to submit for *Love Island*, I went out to lunch with friends and for the first time drank in a way that wasn't about diversion, as I had been doing, but annihilation. (With the exception of the first few weeks, I'd generally been trying to take care of myself by not getting hammered and sometimes doing three to four hours of yoga a day. Although, that often amounted to me just lying on the floor crying – the only thing that made it 'yoga' was the fact that I was wearing Lululemon pants). Ten hours later, I found myself trying to pick up a gentleman I'd once been very keen on. He was in a relationship. I don't remember any of it but when I checked my phone the following morning, my midnight apology text made it very clear what I'd attempted to do.

I was mortified – a lovely garnish for my cocktail of nausea, self-loathing and anxiety. And there was one more ingredient: I was also angry. The gentleman in question was an old friend who knew what I'd been through, and we'd both been . . . messy in front of each other over the years. If it had been him who'd had to send me the apology, I would have told him not to worry about it – but mine was met with silence. I lay in my bed with my hangover, staring at the ceiling, examining our supposed friendship.

It didn't take long before I was thinking of other men in my life and how they'd behaved towards me, and before I knew it I was looking back over my entire history with the opposite sex. I really do mean all of it. I thought about Dad, my brother Niall, boys I'd known as a teenager and at university, men I'd had crushes on, guys I'd worked with and/or fucked in the comedy scene, my relationships, ALL OF IT, and, SPOILER ALERT, it was terrible! It was a miracle I didn't spend the rest of the day with my head in the toilet bowl, not just because of the booze, but because of the crushing realisation that many, many men had made it pretty clear, one way or another, that they hadn't been interested in buying whatever it was I was selling.

How had I not seen this before? If I'd had the same results while pursuing a hobby that I'd had with men, a friend would have taken me in hand by now. They would have sat me down and said, 'Jude, all the time, the effort, the heartache . . . maybe you're just not cut out for glassblowing?' I would've argued with them: 'What do you mean? I love glassblowing. My whole life I've believed that the one thing that will make me truly happy is glassblowing, and society told me this as well. Are you trying to tell me that ALL THIS TIME I SHOULD HAVE BEEN LEATHER CARVING?'

That friend would've been right, though; the overwhelming evidence suggested that I should just forget about dating and embrace a single life with gusto.

It also occurred to me, as I lay in my bed wondering if I was going to heave, that exploring my entire history with the male gender might be a rich stand-up topic. Excessive alcohol consumption really is my muse. While the thought

INTRODUCTION

of doing comedy about it all made me feel even sicker, I'd never felt quite so compelled to go through with something. That feeling outlasted the hangover. A couple of weeks later, I bought the Spirax notebook factory and wrote down every single bad experience I'd ever had with a man.

The premise of the show was to get the audience to decide, after hearing my recollections, whether I should ever date again. It was called *Judith Lucy versus Men*, and as I suspected, it was one of the hardest things I've ever done. But it was also the beginning of turning my life around.

The most difficult aspect was trying to figure out what part I'd played in it all. How much of this was on me? I'd made terrible choices and I'd ignored warning signs – did I actually think that I deserved no better? I have a good career and great friends; it's not like I'd been self-destructive in *every* part of my life, but the truth was that when it came to men, I was apparently willing to put up with a lot of crap. I've never understood gambling – we all know that the house ultimately wins – and I'd always thought, Why put yourself through that? But it seemed I was more than willing to risk my heart and self-worth, in a way that I would never have risked my bank balance. (Although my wallet did often take a hit as well; in fact, if you're a financial adviser, I'd probably stop reading now because you'll just find my monetary history too upsetting.)

Before the relationship that resulted in my wanting to leave planet Earth, I'd been single for six years and had been wondering if the jig might be up for me on that score, and

I'd pretty much come to terms with that. Or so I believed – yet here I was, despairing about being alone again. But this time I wasn't thirty-nine, I was forty-nine, and staring down the barrel of being single FOREVER.

I'm a smart, independent feminist, how had all this *happened*? How had I come to the point where my whole world seemed to have come undone? This was hardly my first broken heart but it was overwhelming in a way I hadn't encountered before, because I was having to concede that, deep down, I'd always been waiting for a man to 'complete me'. So what now – did I have a hole? If a penis wasn't going to fill it, what was? Sweet Jesus, was I going to start gardening? Was my emergency contact from here on in going to be another spinster? Was I going to join a book club, take up bridge and start volunteering somewhere? WAS I GOING TO BUY A CAT?

I couldn't have been more freaked out, but thank god I was so royally fucked over because it completely illuminated what I had to change about my life. I actually mean that. The relationship that I thought was the best thing that had ever happened to me turned into the worst thing, which wound up turning into the best thing again, because without it I wouldn't be where I am now and I like where I am.

Annoyingly, I've had to revisit ground I thought I'd well and truly covered, because I finally understood what the fundamental question was: why had I thought a relationship was the answer to everything? Was it my childhood that had led me to think this? Why had I been drawn to

INTRODUCTION

so many bell ends? And what was I going to do now? If I figured out what had gone wrong, what might my life look like if it was going right? This may sound crazy but I'd never done that before: considered what I wanted from my life without anyone else in it. I've learned a lot. But, also, annoyingly, I don't think the learning ever ends. I don't think you ever get to a place where you dust yourself off and say, Right, thanks universe, no more lessons for me! I've totally got this and now I'm going to open a bowling alley!

It will all fall apart again because that seems to be what happens, just when you think you've worked it all out. But right now? Well, right now, I'm tickety-boo.

Part One

How the Fuck Did I Get Here?

1

Can I Blame My Parents for Everything?

I needed to sort my life out but before I could do that, I needed to do the mature thing and find someone to blame.

Fortunately I'm adopted, so I can point the finger at TWO sets of parents for screwing me up. I had a lot to work with. Both my fathers were absent to some degree. My mothers didn't have much luck with men either, and neither of them wound up having the life they'd expected. There's your explanation! Phew!

THE END

Alright, I think I'm contractually obligated to string this out for another seventy thousand words, so let's begin by really getting down and dirty with nature versus nurture. Let's not. While I would love to make a ton of money by solving that argument once and for all, I have to admit I have no idea what was genetically handed to me and what was absorbed from Ann and Tony Lucy. I'm not dismissing the pivotal role played by *I Dream of Jeannie* and *Gilligan's Island* either. (For years I thought the way to catch a man was by calling him Master, along with baking coconut-cream pies and wearing my hair in pigtails. Granted, it worked a treat in the boudoir.) Still, if I was trying to understand how I'd wound up believing that meeting the man of my dreams was my *raison d'être*, my early years were certainly worth some re-examination. Of course, I knew that my parents had had more of an impact on me than Larry Hagman but it wasn't until after the break-up, when I looked back wondering how I'd arrived here, that I understood just how indelible the mark they left on me was.

I don't know what kind of legacy resulted from being raised by people who weren't biologically connected to me. I've certainly heard that it can make you either shun intimacy or chase it desperately, but a lot of people who weren't handballed to another couple at birth suffer from these tendencies too, so fucked if I know. I'm certainly not denying that being adopted has had an effect on me, but at fifty-two I really can't be arsed thinking about it anymore. (See my first book, *The Lucy Family Alphabet*. Please, I really need to keep the royalties ticking over.)

Do I blame my mothers for my romantic history? It's been frustrating, ladies. I know how to clean my toilet and put on a show, but I just can't roll up my sleeves and make a guy fall in love with me. I can't follow a recipe and end up with a delicious bowl of man pasta. My mothers – Mum, the woman who raised me, and Jan, the woman who gave birth to me – didn't have much luck with their own guy fettuccine/bloke agnolotti/dude lasagne (I'll stop now). Mum spent most of her life chasing the love of an emotionally distant man and Jan didn't wind up with any bloke at all, and doesn't know who my father is. I know this bothers her a great deal more than it does me. When I heard, before I actually met her, that there were two options (this was included in the basic information I was initially given about my birth parents) I was actually thrilled that my birth mother had put it about. I hoped she'd enjoyed herself. But while I'd naively thought, Mum was a bit loose, GREAT, I can now see that for a Catholic woman in the late sixties, the inability to confidently fill out a birth certificate would have seemed like a punishment.

The only aspect of it that irks me is not knowing anything about my father. It's hard for me to grasp that he even exists, or did at some point. There could very well be some silver-haired, bridge-playing, Liberal-voting Liberace fan wandering around out there who makes up, genetically, half of me. Or is he a bald, poetry-reading wizard? Maybe he dyes his hair, recently became vegan and is obsessed with Dwayne 'The Rock' Johnson movies? Maybe he's in prison? What if he lives in a bus and wears harem pants? A friend of mine once dated a guy like that. His attire bothered me, but as not as much as the fact that he lived somewhere without a toilet.

Jan told me my father is either an engineer with whom she had a relationship or a man who was a one-night stand. Jigsaw (an organisation that helps birth parents and children find each other if both parties are interested) has already approached the engineer. He maintains he only slept with one other woman apart from his wife and that wasn't my birth mother, so he refused to take a DNA test. My guess is that he just couldn't be bothered; apparently the least cooperative people in the whole adoption journey are older men who are potential fathers. It seems old codgers just want to hang out in the shed and worry about their enlarged prostate, not deal with surprise offspring.

I've known that I was adopted for twenty-six years now and I've only occasionally wanted to know who my birth father is. I'm lucky enough to have a great relationship with Jan and largely that's been more than enough for me. I'd honestly be happy with just a few facts about my birth dad: health, work, hobbies, little bit of history. It's bizarre not to have the kind of information that (I'm assuming) most people take for granted. I thought about hiring a private investigator and even considered going on *Who Do You Think You Are?* to solve the mystery, but I never acted on any of it. Even if I did work out who he was, it seems unlikely he'd still be alive. So I'll probably never know what he's passed onto me apart from a feeling of unfinished business. (Recently, I heard a story about a woman who was sent a photo of the birth father she'd never met. She showed it to her boyfriend, who took one look at it and said, 'My god, what am I doing at a disco in the eighties?' The likeness was so uncanny that she's shut the door on her interest in her dad for now, lest her mind gets even more blown. To quote Freud, 'That is some freaky shit.')

I haven't completely given up, though. Partly inspired by a friend's success and partly by the feeling that time was running out, in 2018 I spat into a plastic tube and sent it off to Ancestry.com. Coincidentally, it was the same day I put faecal samples in a plastic tube so that the government could hopefully tell me I didn't have bowel cancer. I was pretty curious about both sets of results. My guts were clear, although since I did have to have a colonoscopy, that experience has so far been the more confronting of the two. It would be nice if feedback about potential relatives also involved the drug Propofol.

Initial results from the saliva were fairly predictable – my ethnicity is nearly sixty per cent Irish, and a bunch of distant cousins on Jan's side were unearthed. I'm also twelve per cent European Jewish, so *mazel tov!* Two hopes emerged: that more would come to light about my father (I'm not saying I want reviewers to call this book an electrifying page-turner, but read on!), and I'd never have to have a camera shoved up my coit again.

Jan, my biological mum, hadn't been difficult to find at all, thanks to her registering with the Department for Child Protection when I was nineteen. How different your life must be when you never have to consider that a couple of pina coladas and a roll around in the back of a car might result in another human. It's not uncommon for relinquishing mothers to wind up alone, and Jan never married or had any other children, even though she told me she'd always pictured herself with a husband and five kids, like her sister. When I consider that being single and childless still holds some stigma today, I marvel at her decision. I know she fell in love a couple of times but it just didn't work out.

We're all just a crazy chowder made up from the scallops and carrots of our childhood, aren't we? Of course, I've wondered what I would be like if I'd been brought up by Jan – I very much doubt that 'comedian' would've popped up in my chunky fish soup if she'd been doing the cooking. (My material would have been terrible: 'Did you hear the one about the well-adjusted, socially competent, happy nurse who was an excellent parent?') I've also wondered what effect being raised by a single mother would have had. What if I'd grown up in a household without a man, and where the woman was the breadwinner and had a life of friends and possibilities? Maybe if Jan had been my role model, I would've craved those things less, but as it was, Ann Lucy made me desperate for them.

I have a cardboard box of letters and other keepsakes from my dead parents. It also includes Niall's eulogy for Mum, a beautiful speech that he agonised over and which contains these lines: 'In her youth, Mum had the glamorous looks of a movie star, and throughout her life she remained a very intelligent woman. Being smart and beautiful is supposed to guarantee success and happiness. But the generation and culture my mother was born into made it almost impossible for her to establish an identity outside the home.'

Among the letters are all those Mum wrote me after my sister-in-law broke the news that I was adopted, following a horrendous family fight on Christmas Day when I was twenty-five. They're hard to read, so full of apologies for not having told me herself, and for not saying that she loved me often enough, because 'you see I have been chasing Dad's love – what a hopeless task . . .'

Ann Lucy was my exemplar of womanhood and I wanted my life to be the polar opposite of hers: I wanted a career, independence and friends. I didn't want kids. I did want a man but I wanted an identity very much outside the home. I didn't know it at the time, but I wanted Jan's life.

My parents fought often because of the love Ann Lucy so desperately wanted from her husband. In the last years of her life she actually got it, and had that happened earlier, she might have seen that it wasn't enough and lived her life differently. Instead, when I was a child, getting Dad's attention was my mother's obsession. Her frustration meant that she cried and screamed at him almost nightly. Dad's drinking and money were favourite topics, but she could become hysterical over a disagreement about tinned pineapple or a question like 'Is winter the best season?' None of this had the slightest effect on my father, although it did succeed in making our household a pretty miserable place. I vowed that this life would never be mine.

Dad's dismissiveness actually made me think Mum was weak. I see now that she was simply fighting for the recognition of her partner the only way she knew how. She had no authority, so what else could she do but insist on not being taken for granted, especially when she'd left her homeland of Ireland for this man and supported him while he studied accountancy. When he'd finished his degree he wouldn't allow her to work; he didn't like her having friends and so her whole world was her husband and her children. It now strikes me that she was asking very little from her partner. All she wanted was some acknowledgement of her worth and maybe the odd bunch of flowers and a dinner date. I can only assume that my father felt that being the wage-earner and keeping up home repairs should've made it obvious he cared. Maybe in his head he thought, Well, of course I love you. I'm cleaning the pool filter.

I can't believe that at the time, I thought Mum was the unreasonable one. I wanted her to just be quiet so we could enjoy *Sale of the Century* in peace, not have to witness another screaming match. I loathe any kind of conflict but few things make me more uncomfortable than seeing a woman lose her shit over a man. I can't even watch TV shows or films where a lady howls, is portrayed as 'irrational' or wants revenge. I can happily sit through the Russian roulette scene in *The Deer Hunter* without batting an eyelid, but when I recently saw a BBC drama where a wronged lady turned up at her cheating ex-husband's wedding, I needed a Valium sandwich to get through it. I've never turned up anywhere I wasn't wanted, or made any type of fuss when it comes to men – and now I wish I had.

Sure, I'm reasonably glad that I haven't stabbed anyone or crushed a guy's head with a breadmaker, but why didn't I ever say ANYTHING? Wrapping myself in the cloak of dignity did little for my self-esteem, it was just the excuse I used to deny my anger and sadness in so many situations with so many men.

It also meant that they just didn't even notice I was upset. If I contacted half the guys who I feel treated me badly, or were at least extremely careless with my heart, most of them would be surprised to hear it. God, I'd love to believe that a few of them figured it out, but even then they probably would have thought about it for two seconds before thinking, I'm hungry, or, Maybe I'll just rub one out before the news starts.

I'll always remember a male comedian holding up the front page of a newspaper onstage and gleefully reading out an article about scientists who had done a study which proved that when men were asked, 'What are you thinking?' and they replied, 'Nothing', it was true. I wasn't sure whether I was more alarmed by the finding itself or the comedian's apparent delight in the fact that if you hooked a man's brain to a monitor, all you'd get is flat-lining and one long atonal noise. In retrospect, maybe what I really should've been worried about was that, at the time, I was in love with this man.

That was in my twenties, in the days when I was still attracted to men like my father – though not physically, I hasten to add. Many dads of that time weren't around much, but mine was absent in other ways too. Here's how Niall described him in his eulogy for Mum: 'There were times when he was so utterly disconnected from what most of the rest of us would call reality that it was as if he'd just dropped in from another planet.' That could actually explain why I've never met Mr Right; I've never met anyone from Mars, although I suspect Dad came from the depths of Uranus. Maybe that remoteness is one of the reasons why I don't feel closer to my father since his death, whereas my relationship with Mum is ongoing.

I know almost nothing about Dad's childhood or his parents. There was family wealth, somehow lost but which definitely contributed to his enormous ego. I'll never really know to what extent growing up male in Ireland at a time when it was impossible not to be affected by the civil war informed who he was. I do know that by the time I came along, he lived his life like a less attractive Don Draper. He smoked, drank, fucked around and essentially did what he liked. I doubt it would've occurred to him that he might be engaging in these pleasures to repress his vulnerabilities and doubts about the masculine role he'd been handed. Possibly it did and maybe he was, but it's as though he chose to double down on his machismo. He seemed to love his position of detachment and it made him irresistible. We all wanted to please him. It was an interesting technique; he ran the household by not caring. I'm assuming *that's* why I've found emotionally withholding, charming, funny, womanising alcoholics so attractive. It was a brick wall that I kept dashing my heart against until I was well into my thirties.

I want to give my father the benefit of the doubt: he was a product of his generation, the personification of what society would have deemed A Man. I'm sure he completely believed that (outside his own desires) what mattered most was being a provider. Doubtless he was frustrated that he didn't earn more money, and that when he ventured out on his own his business failed. But it's guesswork: I've no idea what his inner life was like. I never saw him cry. My brother heard him weep when Dad called to tell him that his first marriage had ended, but neither of us quite bought it; we put it down to aging, even though he was only in his late sixties. (Or possibly the conversation coincided with Tony Lucy realising he'd just run out of brandy, which he used to put in his chicken Cuppa Soup.) Maybe he sensed that, thanks to a massive heart attack around a decade earlier, he might not live long enough to see his son and grandson thrive again.

He didn't, in fact, live much longer, and was estranged from both Niall and me when he died. My brother had taken my side when Dad and I had a nonsensical falling-out over a joke I cracked onstage about testicles. For once, the story was actually referring to someone else's father (that's a lesson learned: only ever crack jokes about your own father's scrotum), but for some reason Dad chose to take it to heart, in a way that was quite out of character. I think he was desperately unwell and wanted to hit out at someone. He disowned me by fax, ahead of a show, and thanks to a collision of shock and anxiety, I had a horrendous panic attack onstage for the first time. But it wasn't the last: they persisted for years. My astrology-loving friend Sue says my biggest 'spiritual wound' is about men rejecting me, and while there have been some serious contenders Dad still wins the award. Come on, fellas! Try a little harder, someone needs to dump me with a couple of emojis – maybe a thumbs-down and a smiling turd.

Twenty years after Dad's death, in another first, I found myself wondering about my father's last thoughts. He'd died in bed, lurched forward – it looked like he'd been trying to get up, probably to get my mother. I wondered if he'd thought of his children at the end and, if so, whether those thoughts had been affectionate or regretful. Knowing Dad, though, they were probably more along the lines of, 'Fuck, I may as well have put some more brandy in my chicken Cuppa Soup last night because I think I'm having a heart —' And maybe he hadn't been trying to get to his wife after all; he may have figured that he could punch out one more dart before the Reaper made sure he gave up smoking for good.

While I'll never know his opinion of me at the end of his life, I do know that he generally thought I was funny.

He might even have thought I was smart, although I don't think that characteristic is particularly valued in women even now, let alone when my father was growing up. But a sense of humour definitely had currency in our household. Niall and I loved making each other and our father laugh. Jokes were one of the few ways you got his attention.

I have no memory of him telling me I was pretty, or ever taking an interest in my dating life, though I'm sure he would've presumed that I'd ultimately get married and have kids. Then again, Dad just wasn't all that interested in what the earthlings were up to, even those related to him. Not growing up thinking you're attractive is probably nowhere near as bad as what Mum had to contend with: constantly being reminded, especially by her own mother, of how beautiful she USED to be. So, Ann Lucy never told me that I was beautiful either. I don't mean to harp on about this, I'm just struck by how today's parents tell their kids they're gorgeous even if they've given birth to a bat. I think my generation largely grew up with parents who, thanks to their own upbringings, thought it was far more useful to dwell on their children's shortcomings. I didn't need to waste time discovering that I couldn't sing, for example – Mum had repeatedly told me that already, often when I was just making myself a delicious pressed chicken sandwich.

If only my parents had greeted my every morning with, 'What would you like for breakfast, Aphrodite (or even Cheryl Ladd)?' But as it was, I never thought that looks were where my appeal lay and I clocked every time that impression was reconfirmed. Such as when a schoolfriend told me I wasn't attractive but had a great personality. Dad loved that friend and kept telling me so, long after I stopped having anything to do with her. I found myself wanting to ask, 'Did you actually like her, Dad? Or did you just want her to blow you?' All the boys loved her for the same predictable reasons my father did: she was blonde, had incredible breasts and wore a lot of makeup. My mother despised her because she hated any female Dad liked, including Shirley Bassey.

I did love my father. Right now, I'm still angry at how he treated all of us but especially Mum, because that became how we all treated her. If Mum was interested in something, it was automatically undervalued in our household. I've only considered this recently and thought about the toll it must have taken on her self-worth. She sought fulfilment by trying her hand at everything from macramé to a creative writing course, but I can now see that my brother and I took our cues from Dad, who treated her hobbies as the indulgences of a child.

The most obvious example of this was not a pastime of Mum's but a passion: Catholicism. We were a Catholic family and when I was younger we all went to church, I thought grudgingly – but now I see that once again, this was Dad's attitude, not Mum's. Probably because of my schooling more than anything, up until a certain age I thought that going to Mass should at least be respected, but I still got the message that my mother's faith and belief system wasn't to be taken seriously, as with everything else about Ann Lucy. And despite her intelligence, she wasn't funny, unlike the rest of us. Now I see that our jokes were yet another way she was excluded.

My father's idea of a good time – drinking, smoking, sex, laughing and work – became mine, as did his dismissal of my mother's emotions and interest in anything other than the here and now. My father had all the power in our household and seemed to have all the fun too, so it appears I wanted to be him as well as date him. Not only is that creepy but it turned out to be a contradiction: I had no idea that men like my father are not remotely interested in women like that. They want women like my mother, not her frustration and intelligence but certainly her beauty and devotion. I didn't have the first and I had no interest in gaining the second.

Old habits die hard and my mother's love for my father extended even beyond the grave, as she made clear in a letter she wrote me two weeks before she died. 'Now Judith, when God calls me, I don't want you to grieve and be very unhappy. For a long time, I have had no life – only an existence. I am constantly in pain, my eyesight is nearly gone and I keep having one infection after another, in truth, it [death] would be a relief for me! So be happy that I will again be with Dad.'

This despite the fact that towards the end of her life Mum discovered feminism, and when my father died appeared to be one of those women who got a second lease on life. Unfortunately, by then her own health was failing, so she outlived him by only ten months and, at the end, looked forward to spending all of eternity with the charismatic misogynist who had made much of her life miserable. I guess she felt not even Heaven would be fun if you're a spinster. Mum made it pretty clear in the letter that she hoped her daughter wouldn't meet that fate either: 'If Gavin is the one, then may God bless you both. If not, be assured that Mr Right will come along.'

I'm afraid he hasn't, Mum, and the name of the man I was seeing was Gareth. At least she got one consonant and one vowel right, although that wouldn't have got her very far on *Wheel of Fortune*.

The letter actually says much that I treasure, but I wish it hadn't encouraged me to repeat the same mistake she had made: wasting a lot of time on a man (or in my case, men). I think my mother knew, in the end, that's what she'd done with her life, but how can I knock her for still believing in the fairytale of finding contentment in the arms of a man when after many years and countless fuck-ups I've finally understood that I believed it too?

I wish I'd recognised when she was alive how much more there was to my mother than her relationship with my father. Tucked away in the box with Mum's letters is a certificate (I dimly recall that it was all part of the funeral service) that tells me her life has been memorialised by a tree planted by Men of Trees, whose motto is *Floreant in aeternum arbores* (the forest is eternal). Ann's been dead for twenty years now and I'm sure that the tree would be worth visiting especially because we now know that, thanks to humanity's recklessness, no forest is safe. I don't know how I feel about the tree-planters inserting their gender into the issue but I'm sure Mum would have liked the idea that a bloke had planted something for her. It's only now that I can see that my mother, who loathed housework, enjoyed growing things. She may have skewered her foot on a rake and constantly seemed to have an infected thumb, but that must have been due to liking having her hands in the dirt. The house might have been filthy and a weevil paradise but her handiwork was everywhere outside, and she was equally skilled at growing roses as she was rhubarb.

I was way too busy trying to avoid my life by watching hour upon hour of television to pick up on this. She could have walked into the house with a homegrown potato the size of a bathtub and I just wouldn't have noticed unless she'd been Maxwell Smart. Mum was so ubiquitous that you just took her for granted and never really considered why she did anything. Not long before she died, she talked about wanting to work with Aboriginal women. I've no idea what she meant by that but she'd always been left-leaning, for reasons other than just irritating my father, and she really did want to help make the world a bit better. I remember being impressed that she actually wanted to go out in it, because for so long her life had been so small. In the end, it was another unfulfilled dream.

The older I get, the more I feel that I understand my mother, partly because I'm now experiencing things she went through that I couldn't have grasped as a child. Like menopause: now I see why she wanted the air conditioner on all the time and why her foundation poured off her even as she was applying it. I get that her mood swings and tears weren't just about Dad. I appreciate why she was so freaked out about growing older. No wonder she lied about her age and dieted constantly. Her looks had completely defined her and she believed (probably correctly) they were the main reason her husband had chosen her. And despite all her study and other attempts to find, well, herself, I don't believe that anything mattered to her as much as being a wife.

I now see what a combination I am of my two mothers: I have Mum's craving for Mr Right and Jan's independence, and perhaps it doesn't matter what was in my DNA and what is a reaction to Ann's life. Who on earth came up with the idea that women can have it all? Both of my mothers paid a price for their choices. Ann Mary and Jan Mary, two sides of the same coin, both with the middle name of the ultimate Christian mother. Jan got the career and freedom, but had to live with the consequences of relinquishing her child. Ann got the husband and child, but so much of her potential went unrealised. I am all of this plus my dad and whatever my birth father threw into the mix.

I don't blame any of them for anything, although I sometimes wish I could talk to Mum and Dad about what had made them who they were, try to unravel it all from the beginning. But I know that'd be a hopeless task, a bit like opening a never-ending set of babushka dolls. I do believe in trying to understand the part childhood has played in forming the adult self (I also don't want the therapists' union to put a hit out on me), but there comes a point when you have to let it go. I don't want to be bitching about my father while a nurse is wiping my arse and asking me why I've hidden my hearing aids in my slippers again.

Luckily, in my case it's been easy to let that part go because I know that everything is really my brother Niall's fault.

2
Actually, He Was Quite Heavy
Unpacking My Big Brother

Niall was the most important man in my life. For at least the first fifteen years of my existence, I simply worshipped him. Early on he informed my taste in everything from songs to sitcoms, and as we got older he became an example of how I didn't want to live my life, and I'm not just referring to his early love of Jethro Tull.

Niall was smart, funny and very, very cool (once he got over his love for the Tull). This might have made some parents proud but unfortunately that wasn't Tony Lucy's jam – instead, he was threatened. A friend once told me about his father and one of his brothers getting drunk enough to flop out their penises and compare them. Admittedly, Mum was always telling me that my labia majora would never be as big as hers but I guess women are just naturally competitive. (Fun genital fact: did you know the clitoris never ages?

So Grandma might have forgotten where she's put her cup of tea but she's rocking the clit of a twenty-year-old!)

The Lucy men never did anything so gauche as to actually compare schlongs, although Dad often had the metaphorical ruler out, and as Niall became an adult the major arguments shifted from being between our parents to being between him and Tony Lucy. For my father to need to prove himself constantly against Niall there must have existed a strong streak of insecurity under his arrogance. Of course, this had consequences. My brother maintained that he didn't shed a single tear after Dad died. I believed him. Dad once told me, in a rare moment of insight possibly inspired by his fourth glass of flagon riesling (or was he just trying to justify his treatment of my brother?), that he was hurt when as a teenager Niall stopped turning to him for advice, presumably because he was becoming his own person. Their relationship didn't really recover. It was something that was going to repeat itself.

I don't know what Niall was like as a kid; he was twelve when I was born. It's hard for me to imagine him as a vulnerable little boy who loved footy, the anime cartoon *Marine Boy* and his dog, Tong. My brother told me about the terrible fights Mum and Dad used to have, not that I missed out on that treat altogether, but they seemed a tad less dramatic by the time I came along. I have no memory of Mum ever leaving Dad, for example, something she did several times when I was a baby. It's like their dramas became less *Dynasty* and more *Home and Away*, possibly because they were older or maybe Ann just became more resigned. I very much suspect that Niall was a pawn in that game. I doubt that even our father would have been competing with his pre-adolescent son, but because Niall often saw Dad drunk and Mum upset, it's not hard to guess whose side he would have been on. While my brother never stopped loving our mother, I think as he got a little older her impotence in the face of our father disheartened him. He had to be there for her but why wasn't she ever there for him? I've pieced this theory together recently based on Niall's treatment of her in later life, which seemed to be the result of both affection and rage.

A few months before Mum died, we had to put her in an aged-care facility. Her ongoing ill health meant that she needed access to medical treatment around the clock. We would visit her, and Niall, apart from a greeting and a farewell, would stand in the corner and not speak. It was really something; Mum and I would be jabbering away uncomfortably, both painfully aware of his silence. He may as well have painted himself gold, put a cap on the floor for coins and posed on a box. (I've always been intrigued by living statues. 'What's your talent?' 'Standing so still that a pigeon shits on me.' 'How proud your parents must be.') I think he loved her enough never to let her down but was angry enough to be incapable of anything but the bare minimum, including showing any affection.

In one of her letters to me Ann mentions that she came to rely on Niall as the male of the house because Dad simply wasn't present in any sense. I think she turned to her son with her problems and also simply for company. What a burden for a teenager. Kids don't understand how adult relationships work either, especially between their parents. A bad argument can make them think a marriage is over *forever*. When my mother went so far as leaving my father those times when I was a baby, he probably knew she would never walk away for good from the man she adored. My brother didn't know that, though, and must have found those walkouts terrifying and confusing. It makes sense to me that, having grown up in a household like that, you would want to lock everything down when you could, and in later life, being in control became very important for Niall.

By the time I have memories of him, my brother was fully formed. He loved movies and reading but his biggest passion was music. I suspect his role model was the 24-year-old Bob Dylan captured in the documentary *Don't Look Back*. When I saw the film, I couldn't believe how comfortable the singer was in his own skin at such a young age. His lack of interest in everyone around him meant they all tried to impress him. I found his arrogance amusing when he was dealing with the much less gifted singer Donovan, but was pissed off when his treatment of his girlfriend, Joan Baez, wasn't much better. I'm pretty sure that my brother, like a lot of people, would have thought Dylan's talent gave him licence to do whatever he wanted. We tolerate a lot from geniuses. And who am I kidding? As if I wouldn't have thrown myself at a 24-year-old Dylan. (Although I probably would have tried to bang Donovan too and possibly even Neil Sedaka.)

Niall's love of the humanities and art certainly set him apart from Dad, an accountant whose interest in creative endeavours began and ended with his Neil Diamond record collection and his passion for *Starsky and Hutch*. They did, however, share a love of sport, booze and smoking. Guy stuff. Like Mr Dylan, they also had very healthy egos. But Tony Lucy's self-importance was primal, whereas I suspect my brother's was a defence mechanism – partly a result of Dad's competitiveness but partly just because he was an Australian male, who probably had to do a little overcompensating for the fact that his interests would eventually lead him to a career in academia and not, say, professional cricket or woodchopping.

Niall looked after me as a small child, and gave me a feeling of security in that unpredictable household that no one ever gave him. While he had interests and friends I think his real escape was what wound up defining him: being cool. Cool puts you above other people – it allows you to judge them and it means you're never exposed or out of control. It gives you strict guidelines to live by: the right music, art, clothes. Smoking used to be cool, as was drinking if you could hold it. I would never describe Tony Lucy as cool but his detachment from life conveyed something of this quality, and Christ knows, he could hold his piss. Mum didn't tick any of those boxes. She was messy, emotional, loud and embarrassing. Cool is largely a male domain (you can't be cool while you're having a baby or changing a tampon; I did once hear of an artist smoking a cigarette with her vagina, but I don't think that's quite the same thing) and it takes work.

My brother spent a lot of time on his image. I remember him perfecting his handwriting by choosing the best cursive version of each letter and then practising them for weeks. But that had nothing on the effort he put into his hair. I'm confident Jerry Hall has spent less time on that part of her grooming. In later years, when he finally let it go grey, Niall's thick locks grew very long. I mentioned this after not having seen him for a while and he said, 'It's the "I don't give a fuck" look.' When the hair changed he started to wear more suits, but essentially from the neck down it was always black jeans, boots and retro shirts. He went kayaking in that outfit. I'm not making that up. It's hard to know what would have offended my brother more, ordering a non-alcoholic drink in a bar or wearing a pair of shorts, anywhere. Knees were simply not part of his world.

As a little kid, I loved having such a groovy sibling, not least because I knew this smart, intimidating guy thought his funny, not very cool sister was great. Niall spent a lot of time with me when we were younger – he read to me and took me for walks and when I got a bit older he took me to movies, plays and bands. He supported my interest in performing and was a fount of advice and wisdom on everything from my wardrobe to what my life would be like after school. He made living in our household bearable.

ACTUALLY, HE WAS QUITE HEAVY

Unfortunately, this all began to change when I turned fifteen and started having opinions of my own. (Sound familiar?) Our relationship was at its optimum when I was his acolyte and just did whatever he wanted. By mid-adolescence, hanging out with him and his girlfriend was becoming a little less fun. The two of them moved to Sydney when I was sixteen, and while visiting them was in theory wonderful, all I remember about those holidays is feeling tense. There was a particular way of doing everything and taste was crucial. The same exacting standards that applied to culture also applied to the people they knew, and I was constantly in fear of making a mistake. This was partly in my own head of course, although it wasn't like I thought he'd stop loving me if I bought a Wa Wa Nee album (actually, that would have been fair enough), but his approbation just meant so much to me. At the time, I put most of this down to his girlfriend because I didn't want anything to taint my feelings for my beloved big brother. I didn't really start to reassess this until that relationship ended and he married his first wife because while the women had changed, my brother's behaviour hadn't.

Thankfully, with Niall in another city I could blossom into the performer/wanker I am today! He always backed my choices but would probably have raised an eyebrow at my pursuit of public speaking and debating. And his whole face would have fallen off when I went to a Christian Youth Camp and had sincere conversations about Jesus and abortion. Admittedly, I went largely in the hope of getting a pash, but it didn't take me long to realise that the boys who attended these gatherings were even more desperate than the girls. The priest started looking really attractive – actually, so did the industrial-sized container of margarine I saw in the kitchen.

When I was in my forties, Niall told me I was loud when I was a teenager. I was genuinely surprised: I remember trying to be especially quiet around him, not because I was worried about upsetting him, but so as not to appear in any way like Mum. As he got older, Niall's moods became more intense and his presence as dominating as Dad's. Niall trumped his father, though – while he could be just as emotionally remote, he was smarter and had turned himself into the arbiter of taste and behaviour. He was never going to feel vulnerable or impotent again; now, he was calling the shots.

The closest the adult Niall ever came to those childhood feelings of chaos again was when his first marriage ended. That's when the metamorphosis into Dad really picked up speed, and when my brother put away a piece of himself – the part that could be playful and did not have to control everything – so now there were even more strictures than just being cool. I think he decided he was never going to have his heart broken again, no matter what it took.

A few years after that, I was staying with Niall and his second wife when I was struck by a feeling that I couldn't quite put my finger on. I remember going upstairs to use the toilet and seeing a little caterpillar on the wall. I thought it was cute, until I realised, in a moment not too dissimilar to a scene out of a seventies horror film, that the walls were covered with caterpillars, and, indeed, the whole second storey of the house was infested with moths. What luck that was where I would be sleeping. I went downstairs and said something along the lines of, 'Hey, what's up with the moths?' My brother's slight look of derision suggested that I was the one with the problem. And then it struck me: I hadn't encountered this sort of laissez-faire attitude to infestations and general filth since ... our parents' house. It's fascinating to me what blind spots we have when it comes to repeating the past.

Despite their combined family of three kids, dinner was a quiet, strained affair that reminded me of the joyless meals of my childhood. Later that night, during an argument, my sister-in-law became emotional and my brother remained silent until he finally unleashed his terrifying anger. My god, I thought, the transformation is complete, I'm staying with Mum and Dad. Everything in the household revolved around my brother; like his father, and his favourite troubadour, he was the star of the show.

After my relationship ended, coincidentally at the height of the #MeToo movement, my ex told me that one of the things he thought might help explain his own actions was an apology recorded by Dan Harmon, creator of the TV series *Community*, who had harassed a young female writer. When I read a transcript of his mea culpa, these sentences stood out: 'I certainly wouldn't have been able to do it if I had any respect for women. On a fundamental level I was thinking about them as different creatures. I was thinking about the ones that I liked as having some special role in my life and I did it all by not thinking about it.' I'd never *really* let myself consider this point before – that to some men, women aren't equal fellow humans but something that exists only in relation to them and their desires. These men are the leading actors and we're the supporting bit-players who disappear when we're not involved in the all-important story of their lives. Deep down, I did already know this of course, but hadn't been able to fully admit to myself that the gender I believed held the key to my happiness sometimes didn't view me as quite human. I think that, consciously or unconsciously, some men think this way. I'm not saying they think we're cuttlefish, just slightly lesser versions of them.

I don't doubt that my brother loved me but I was very much a supporting cast member in his movie. For my twenty-first birthday Niall insisted I fly from Melbourne to Sydney and spend it with him and his much older friends at a restaurant, rather than with my own buddies. I had the joy of waking up in my own vomit after a friend's twenty-first but never my own! Then again, I agreed to it.

I honestly don't think my brother consciously understood that he was behaving in this way. But if he was denied a promotion, say, or was having trouble in his marriage, it was assumed that I would drop everything to be there for him. How many times have we seen unmarried ladies expected to fill the role of caregiver, whether in a practical sense or to perform the emotional labour of comforter or problem solver? No one says it out loud but if you're a childless woman, what's your purpose? Surely helping those with families is more important than whatever might be going on in your own life? I'm thinking of getting a torch grafted onto my forehead so at least I'll be handy in a blackout. Childless men aren't viewed in the same way and certainly don't attract the same stigma of failure or selfishness. For women, it doesn't even matter if you're a prime minister, many will still see you as a barren spinster.

The faeces really started to hit the fan in my relationship with Niall when his first wife told me I was adopted. Niall insisted that this fact should make no difference to my life whatsoever, because he didn't want my knowing it to make any difference to his. It had always been Us and Them, Niall and me against Mum and Dad, and I think he feared that this news might change that dynamic. He would barely discuss it with me. Our father had decided that if he were adopted he wouldn't want to know, and therefore couldn't see why I might, and similarly, his son had determined that I should respond in the way he wanted me to; that is to say, like I'd just been told I had a mild allergy to turmeric.

A whole new world had been opened up for me and I wanted a relationship with my birth mother. Niall could never understand this and made things pretty difficult, at one point suggesting that I should plan separate visits to Perth so that when I stayed with him (Niall had moved back from Sydney by this stage), there would be no visits to Jan. That way he could pretend she didn't exist. For a long time, he made it obvious that he didn't want me to even mention her name around him, although as it became clear over the years that our relationship wasn't threatened by this new side to my life, his position began to soften.

Finally, though, we had the falling-out that had been coming for years. I wrote a book about our childhood called *The Lucy Family Alphabet* and wanted him to read the manuscript. I still don't know if he ever finished it, but I do know that he didn't want a light shone on our early years. My way of coping with trauma is by revealing it and his way was to withdraw and repress. The book might have been the catalyst, but as a friend who recently argued with her brother said to me, 'When you argue with your sibling as an adult, it's about your entire history.'

I remember being in the shower at his house and literally trembling with rage that he wouldn't talk about the book. Then it hit me. I didn't have to be there. I could just leave. I could go and stay with Jan or a friend, or even at a hotel! I wasn't a little kid anymore. I'd finally understood, at thirty-nine, that this was about something I no longer needed: his approval.

We didn't speak for two years. If I'm honest, while this made me unhappy and I'll always regret being a terrible aunty during that time, it was also liberating to draw a line in the sand. Then he rang me, on Christmas Day, and I burst into tears and said I was glad he'd called. That's as close as we came to discussing what had happened. I knew his silence was part of my punishment; I had broken with him and he would never completely forgive me for it. While I yearned for the closeness we used to have, I knew that to reclaim it I would basically have to go back to being fourteen, and it would have been too weird to start dressing like Adam Ant again.

And then he got lung cancer. We had about a year with him and I spent as much time in Perth as I could. Some people have tremendous revelations or a spiritual awakening when they know they're dying, and some people continue on exactly as they had before. That was my brother; there were no big discussions, nothing was resolved and I had to bite my tongue almost daily. But it was as if we had returned to our childhood – often we would just sit on the couch watching TV together. When one of his friends said to him, 'It must be so good to have Judith here, even to just hear her voice,' Niall said, 'No, she doesn't need to say anything, she just has to be here.' This made me feel a bit like a human beanbag but I knew what he meant.

His emotional suppression continued to the end. We all had to exist in a horrendous bubble of denial and forced normalcy. Even in his last days, when the cancer had spread to his brain and he struggled to even get off the couch, he wanted to go to the pub to watch a friend, Rob Snarski, play a gig. He became furious when his wife and I stopped him, accusing us of 'ruining his fucking life', but maybe that was just to save face. When Rob, who was staying with him, performed three heartbreaking songs in the living room for the family and some of Niall's other buddies, there wasn't a dry eye in the house – apart from Niall – the music finally giving the rest of us permission to sob.

I still marvel at the fact that we coupled his death with watching the last series of *Breaking Bad* where, yes, Walt, the main character, was also dying of lung cancer. Nobody dared talk about this, either. There was no will, no funeral plan and no goodbyes. I returned home to Melbourne and, despite my then partner, felt the kind of loneliness that suddenly being the last remaining member of your immediate family can bring. At least when my parents died, I could get drunk and ring Niall – but who could I talk to about not being a sister anymore?

Those last twelve months were almost unbearable because so much that I yearned to talk about remained unsaid, yet I'm still glad we had them. I'm grateful that my brother and I just got to hang out. I do wish we'd argued and cried and hugged and worked through all our frustrations with each other, but that was not who he was. There would be no emotions and no mess, all the way to the grave.

He died at home. We took it in turns to sit with his body. I didn't linger. I smelt him, though, because I knew I would remember how he looked and sounded but I wanted to hang onto that aroma that was him and only him, a smell I'd known all my life.

I can't be sure, but I think Niall, like his father before him, saw personal growth as something to be avoided.

ACTUALLY, HE WAS QUITE HEAVY

Firstly, it implied admitting fault, it might even entail *apologising*, which certainly didn't interest the Lucy men. Secondly, and more importantly, it might involve making yourself vulnerable. Better to white-knuckle it and cling onto your unchangeable idea of yourself as a man who's never wrong. Yet if there's one lesson life keeps teaching us, it's that change is not only completely unavoidable, it's essential. My brother, though, had decided it was better to be seen as aloof and cool than a human with feelings. How lonely that must have been. How much beer and how many cigarettes did it take to repress all that?

My brother was the one who introduced me to art, literature and music. What a wonderful gift. But he's probably also why I spent years seeking the approval of straight males and often believed that my life came second. That's not his fault of course. Well, it is, but it's also Mum and Dad's and their parents' and *Cleo* magazine's and *The Benny Hill Show*'s and Aristotle's. In fact, I think I might even put some of the blame on a dude from 4000 BCE in Mesopotamia who wrote 'No Fat Chicks' on an ancient bowl.

I'm still angry with my brother about the mess he left when he died and with some of his behaviour when he was alive, but I know that won't last – I just haven't quite surrendered it yet. One day, I'll only remember how much I love him and how much he loved me. I'll remember days like the one we had in Cornwall, visiting a friend of his first wife's, when Niall feigned illness so that he and I could spend the afternoon and evening in the local pub drinking and laughing until closing. I know that eventually I'll only remember the stories like the one Mum used to love to tell about his first day of school, when he thought lunchtime was the end of the day and walked home a perilously long way all the while clutching a bunch of flowers he'd picked for his mother, he loved her so. I will only remember the sides of my brother that were tender and generous and not cool at all. I miss that person very much.

3
When I Grow Up, I'll Be A Feminist Princess
School, University and, Uh-Oh, Boys

For a long time I said, and completely believed, that I didn't encounter sexism until I moved to Melbourne and started doing stand-up comedy. (Just ignore the previous two chapters of this book, I was actually raised on the archipelagic island Themyscira along with the other Amazons and my buddy Wonder Woman, and yes, I did look incredible in my tiny metallic onesie. Unlike my friend, though, I didn't have an invisible plane, just a superpower called denial.)

I thought this because I went to an all-girls school and then majored in theatre arts at university, which was also dominated by female students. Putting aside the gender-stereotypes bonanza that was going on in my own home, on my TV screen, in my church, my education, and almost everything else I encountered, I'd somehow managed to hide from myself the fact that while I spent my first twenty-odd years working hard and determined to have a career, I was also completely convinced that my 'real' life would only begin once I had a man.

The annoying thing is that I really could've put the whole thing to bed when I was six. We had a handful of boys at my tiny primary school, which I attended until I was nine, and one of them proposed to me in grade one. I turned him down. I wonder if Stuart is still available? I rejected him because his family didn't have a pool. I will regret that decision for the rest of my life. How irritating that my standards peaked when I was still reading about Dick and Dora, Fluff and Nip. I went on to chase men who not only could never have afforded a pool, but who chiefly encountered water as a mixer, and rarely as something to wash clothes, their body or teeth with.

One memory I have of primary school reveals a lot about the year it was implanted, 1972. It's of playing chasey. Despite the fact that the girls out-numbered the boys by about eight to one, the young gentlemen always chased us, not the other way round, and when we were caught they would pull our underpants down. What a lively, innocent introduction to sexual assault! What were the teachers thinking? Were they just too busy sucking on another Alpine Light and discussing the previous night's episode of *Kojak*?

After grade four, boys disappeared until we were fifteen, at which age we had excruciating dancing lessons and socials with our brother school Aquinas. While not unpopular at Santa Maria College, I was never popular with the guys.

I knew our teacher Margot Morcombe was not talking to me when she told our class about the perils of heavy petting. What did that even mean? It sounded like it involved squashing a hamster. Still, her warning was fine with me because I don't remember being remotely attracted to anyone in my year – all the desirable boys were a year or two older, such is the way adolescence launches itself on us. Not that this was an issue for me either, since by then I was well on my way to becoming a trope: the less attractive, brunette, funny best friend that has featured in so many rom-coms.

The girl who told me that I wasn't attractive always had boyfriends. Some were even at university, which, looking back, makes me want to call them and say, 'Hey creep, did you get off on wanting to bang a fifteen-year-old schoolgirl?' Although, I'm sure they'd simply say 'Sure, doesn't everybody?'

(This is even statistically borne out. I read about a dating-app survey which revealed that, in terms of appeal to the opposite sex, men peak at age fifty and women at eighteen, with men up until the age of thirty still messaging teenage girls. I know, why don't we all just kill ourselves now? 'Happy birthday, honey! You're finally an adult, but unfortunately, when it comes to the sexy part of that, men don't actually want adult, they want adolescent. For the love of god, get rid of your pubic hair!' The same article said that men become more attractive the more educated they are, and women less so. Christ, why didn't I leave school when I was eight? I could've been beating them off with a stick.)

Almost every fella my alluring buddy dated claimed that if they hadn't been with her, they would have been with me (my interest in them didn't seem to factor into the equation), although this never eventuated when their relationship ended. I was the best friend with the personality. I was Janeane Garofalo to her Uma Thurman in the movie *The Truth About Cats & Dogs* but I never wound up with the handsome photographer with the heart of gold, Brian, who valued character over beauty, mainly because THAT NEVER HAPPENS IN REAL LIFE. Instead I wound up a stand-up comedian (as is Janeane Garofalo) who drank herself to sleep and screwed a lot of dickwads.

Naturally, when I was at school, I had crushes on pop stars and actors and I remember constantly fantasising about a boy standing behind me and putting his arm around me. That was as racy as it got. (I suppose the equivalent today would be anal sex with some guy choking me out.) Who knows what that was about? Maybe I just had difficulty picturing a face and could only conjure up an arm and a hand, or was it just about affection? I wasn't from a tactile family, so I probably would have been thrilled with a pat on the head or an enthusiastic handshake paired with a sincere 'Peace be with you.'

I did fall in love with my new best friend, Michelle, at fourteen, which was all-consuming. We would give each other cards and poems and go on 'dates'. We had no idea what a lesbian was and I wonder if we would have given it a crack if we had known. I suspect not; we modelled ourselves on the relationship between Sebastian Flyte and Charles Ryder in the BBC's adaptation of *Brideshead Revisited*, which was never consummated. (Now that I think of it, I often resorted to male role models as the female ones just weren't there.) We were living our lives like a 1945 novel that examined family and Catholicism, while other girls were getting fingered.

It's well documented how intense female friendships can be, especially at that age, and maybe nothing I've ever had with a man has lived up to the romance and excitement of that first liaison. I still love Michelle and although that initial intensity of feeling is long gone my gratitude for the ongoing friendship isn't. I'd found someone I really connected with and while I'd had friends before, it wasn't until I met her that I truly understood the importance of having someone outside your family who's in your corner, someone with no obligation to hang out with and support you, who simply likes the cut of your jib. Thank god that was something I worked out relatively early, because without people like Michelle in my life, I might have wound up living in a swamp and talking only to frogs. Although Swamp Lady does have a ring to it, I might have missed out on one of the great joys of life, friendship.

Something else Michelle and I shared was a love of school. We were *those* girls: drama students, public speakers and suckholes. I've joked that I would have been better off smoking and kissing boys, but not only was that not really an option, it also just wasn't me. I liked studying and getting good marks and I knew, even then, that work was going to be important to me. I'd realised this was the way to avoid Ann Lucy's life, and would affirm me in a way that had nothing to do with how I looked. Fortunately, I was also able to use my ability, honed at home, to make people laugh, so I wasn't completely despised for being an academically overachieving goody-goody.

I don't lovingly reflect on my years of Catholic indoctrination but I am grateful for having attended an all-girls school with some terrific teachers who fostered our ambitions. While I'm sure there were pupils in my year who mainly dreamed of becoming a wife and mother, most of the students I liked were smart and wanted careers, and because there were no boys around it never occurred to us that we couldn't do anything we chose to. That's the odd contradiction of an all-girls Catholic school: the religion is deeply misogynist but both our primary- and high-school principals were terrifying nuns who instilled in us a desire to do our very best, whether that was in food and nutrition class (yes, cooking) or physics and chemistry. Like many Catholic girls, I briefly wanted to be a nun when I was a kid, and if I'd been around a few centuries ago and had wanted to study rather than marry, it might have seemed like a pretty great option. I've recently started listening to the music of German nun Hildegard of Bingen of the High Middle Ages, who was a Benedictine abbess, writer, composer, philosopher, mystic and visionary – a polymath in other words. I'm guessing she had more fun than Gerdrut stuck on the farm helping her husband Albrecht clean out the pigsty before giving birth to her sixteenth child and bleeding to death.

My school environment meant it never entered my head that a brain and a sense of humour weren't irresistible traits for any girl to have. What sixteen-year-old boy wouldn't prefer a girl who loved reading Tennessee Williams and could make you laugh to someone called Samantha with big tits? Only the ones, as I later discovered, who hadn't come out yet. I had absolutely no confidence when it came to the opposite sex, but with even the girls in my year who didn't look like Heather Locklear as hot cop Stacy Sheridan on *T.J. Hooker* pairing up, I couldn't quite work out why boys weren't interested in me AT ALL. (I may not have thought I was pretty but Jesus, even the girl who'd shaved her own eyebrows off was getting more action than me.) Still, I wasn't too worried: Niall assured me that my life would change completely once I went to university and met my people, the students I actually had stuff in common with rather than those I'd been forced to swim with in my small Catholic-educated pool.

My brother wasn't the only one giving me revelatory information towards the end of high school: his girlfriend at the time gave me my first ever book on feminism. Unbelievably, I can't remember what it was called. It wasn't one of the classics but it changed my life – that I remember. It was a complete shock to me to learn that women and men weren't treated equally. Admittedly I probably should have picked this up a little sooner, given my household, but by that stage I'd come to understand that a lot of what was happening at 111 North Lake Road, Melville, was odd, so I just added Dad's treatment of Mum to the THEY'RE INSANE list. My world was tiny and largely devoid of males and I genuinely thought that when my actual life began, everyone would be treated the same, wouldn't they? The blinkers fell from my eyes thanks to that book and I was appalled, which was exactly the right way to start university, where most of my beliefs about gender, politics, religion, race and culture were blown apart and it was fantastic!

Considering the progressive ideas that were around then, well over thirty years ago, I remain surprised and disappointed that we're not currently living in Utopia. Coming of age in the eighties, when most of my contemporaries had no interest in marriage and only a latent interest in having children, I believed we'd all be living in a whole manner of exciting ways by now. It would all be about community; friends would be raising children together, while the institution of marriage and gender stereotypes would be dead! Yet these ideas seem as entrenched as ever. I welcome equal marriage rights, I just didn't think anyone would still be interested in any kind of marriage. It's a mystery to me how we can live in a time when, thanks to the LGBTQIA+ community, we are finally starting to embrace different ideas about gender identity, and yet we continue to uphold heterosexual male and female stereotypes. In fact I feel we've gone backwards in that respect, compared to when I was in my twenties. I hope that's because this attitude is in its death throes.

If you had shown my braless, hairy eighteen-year-old self a picture of a Kardashian and told me that women of the twenty-first century would want to look like her I would have rolled my eyes and said, 'Yeah, and I guess some guy who grabs women's pussies is going to be the leader of the free world?' Don't get me wrong, I appreciate that we've come a long way from what Ann Lucy grew up with, but to paraphrase something my friend Kaz Cooke said to me many years ago, I just thought feminism would have a linear narrative.

There weren't that many straight men at university, and of the few available those attracted to me were generally weirdos. I have nothing against weirdos, I am one, but just to give an example, one of them came up to me many years later at a gig and apologised for stalking me. Thankfully his skin had improved; when I first knew him, it had the appearance of red dough – he looked like a day-old beetroot sandwich in a polyester shirt. Another interested university guy was lovely but had an inexplicable lump coming out of his forehead in the shape of a snow dome – you just wanted to turn him upside down and shake him.

As at school, I found myself a friend, Andrea, who non-freaks were attracted to and who had all the attributes I felt I lacked. Andrea was, and remains, funny, smart and gorgeous, and back then she was way more confident with the opposite sex than I was. She'd had sex, boyfriends, and knew what she was doing. I had NO IDEA.

At one point Andrea and I shared a house. It belonged to her much older boyfriend, who couldn't live there because he was dodging debt collectors. Happily, this meant we could stay there for very little rent as long as we watered his dope plants. We were just playing at being adults. We didn't even know how to eat properly – the backbone of our diet was a laxative tea. One evening two very lovely fellow students, Steve and Craig, came over, clearly both extremely keen on Andrea. I think, in what was possibly the closest either of us will ever come to taking part in an orgy, Andrea may have pashed both of them and then actually ordered one of them to kiss me. Yes, it was humiliating and I slunk off to my single bed alone.

Lack of confidence meant I wasn't very proactive, apart from when I asked out an impossibly good-looking guy called Mark. We had a delightful dinner, I bought him a single red rose, and then, of course, he told me he was gay – the first and last time I was attracted to a homosexual.

Except it wasn't. The first man I had a crush on at university was Andrew. Andrew was gay. I'd never met a gay man before – well, of course I must have but I just didn't know they even existed. It seems incomprehensible now but that's how sheltered we were. (At one point our sex education teacher was an actual nun, so I'm surprised that the first time I saw a penis I didn't expect it to look like a bible.) I can't remember when Andrew told me about his sexuality, maybe during one of our long chats in his car when he pulled over just before dropping me home. Nor do I remember when I finally became aware of homosexuality, although I was seeing films like *Querelle* in my late teens so presumably I joined some dots. I was certainly completely unfazed when Andrew told me. For once, I knew that the rejection wasn't about me. This person did really like me – just not in quite the way that I liked him, but I could work with that. We're friends to this day.

Over the years I've fallen for many gay men and I'm happy to say that my little crushes have often transmuted into an enduring reciprocated love. Without wanting to make a sweeping generalisation here (but screw it, the book is full of them) I suspect that the very traits that make me predisposed to having gay male friends and audience members is precisely what straight men are not so drawn to. I'm going to quote Mark Trevorrow (aka Bob Downe) here, who, when asked why gay men like female comedians, said, 'We just like smart, funny women.' I realised this a lot sooner than I realised that straight men often don't.

After Andrew, the next gay man I fell for was Colin, not long after moving to Melbourne. He had a connection with one of my housemates and came to see my first one-woman show at the tiny La Mama theatre. When a group of us headed back to my place, Colin offered to give me a lift. Someone neither of us was particularly fond of was going to follow him, but when we got in the car, Colin cranked up the wonderful Carlene Carter (we share a love of country music and Bruce Springsteen) and said, 'I think we'd better lose her, don't you?' And sped off. I'm not proud of this now but at the time it won me over completely.

I was introduced to Colin while his partner, Tom, was dying of AIDS. I met Tom only once unfortunately, and Colin (one of the smartest people I know, who'd studied drama and graphic design) subsequently dedicated his life to working for organisations related to HIV prevention and sexual health. Not surprisingly he wasn't at his best when our friendship formed. After Tom died, Colin and his new partner, Richard, would often turn up to visit my friend Audrey and me around midmorning with spirits from the bottle shop where they worked, and we would while away the hours drinking cocktails, laughing and crying. I often wound up on Colin's lap during this period, like some sort of horny, drunk ventriloquist's dummy.

The high/low point of this time was when we all went on a mystery flight to Hobart. Everyone was ridiculously drunk for about thirty-six hours and then we continued drinking when we got back to Melbourne ... at the airport. To this day I don't know why we didn't go to a bar instead of choosing to drink somewhere with a name like Air Jet or Fuel. Eventually, Richard was so drunk that he got up on the table and started doing the birdie dance. We were, of course, asked to leave. Never one to take this sort of treatment lying down, Richard insisted on seeing someone in a managerial position to demand whether they had a problem with homosexuals and comedians. We had to make a hasty exit, but somehow he still got us a free bottle of wine.

The gay men that I'm close to all have one thing in common: they are hilarious. Early on in my stand-up journey I worked with one who was funny for a living and who helped turn my career around: Julian Clary.

I'd been doing comedy for two or three years and often my gigs were simply a nightmare. I was generally the only woman on the bill, which meant that I was often ignored by my fellow performers and loathed by the audience. This was particularly the case whenever an international comic came to town. In those days, thanks to our union, the American or English comedian everyone had paid to see had to have two Australian support acts. While it was wonderful to have a gig six nights a week for a decent wage, was it worth the anguish of getting up in front of a crowd who simply couldn't wait for you to finish and who made that pretty clear by talking throughout your entire act or by yelling out something eloquent like 'Fuck off'?

The exception to this rule was when I was asked to support the fabulous Mr Clary. It didn't take too long for straight audiences to discover Julian in Australia but on that first tour his crowd was mostly gay men. The other support act was a very blokey heterosexual man, Tim – a likeable performer and a good stand-up who generally went down very well (a lot better than me in those days). I remember how surprised he was when the audience didn't respond to him. They did, however, respond to me.

I was in heaven. Night after night, when I had the opportunity to either drink with Julian's straight (and attractive) male crew, I opted instead to go out with Mr Clary. I'm fairly confident that the first option would've got me laid but I was far more interested in accompanying Julian to the gay club Three Faces and watching the drag shows. I'll always remember sitting in the balcony as the compere announced that Julian was there and shone a spotlight on him. Unsurprisingly, the crowd went wild! What I wasn't prepared for was the next announcement, 'And we also have another special guest here tonight . . . Judith Lucy,' as the spotlight swung to me. I will never forget it. I may not have been succeeding at meeting my Prince Charming, but during those early years I was discovering the value of platonic love with women and gay men. That love sustains me to this day.

If only I'd been as comfortable with straight men. I had no idea how to flirt, and thanks to Hollywood movies I also assumed that I didn't have to do anything, it wasn't really up to me. I thought love just magically appeared – you just 'knew' when you'd met the right person, as did they. I was a feminist, but wasn't the guy meant to chase you? Surely one of the three attractive heterosexual guys I was studying with would just put down his joint and bucket of chips one day and sing me a sonnet?

For the most part, I was too busy at university to be bothered by being single. I made lifelong friends, had a tremendous time, and of course threw myself into study and acting. I was involved in seventeen plays in two years, occasionally backstage but mostly onstage, and often as the lead. I HAD A BALL! It'd be in the next chapter of my life – a drama school interstate was the dream – that I'd meet the love of my life and become the next Judy Davis.

In fact, I didn't even bother completing my degree (education was always going to be free, wasn't it?) but worked two jobs, seven days a week, to save enough money to move to Melbourne, where I was convinced the Victorian College of the Arts would accept me. I'd also moved back in with Mum and Dad, which was the best motivation for working hard and saving I could've found. Moving back home was unusual then – our generation just couldn't get out fast enough. I know it's a lot more financially challenging for young adults to live independently these days but I still think the main reason we were in a hurry was because our parents were just cunts.

I left my hometown a virgin, but it's worth mentioning for the record that I might have had more opportunities than I realised.

The first gentleman I ever fooled around with was in fact Michelle's brother, Michael. I'd held a torch for him for some time (rather like Charles Ryder's attraction for Sebastian's sister Julia in *Brideshead*) but I never did anything about it because I didn't want her to think that our friendship was in any way the result of that crush. (Have I mentioned that I'm a little bit of an overthinker?) Even back then, I didn't want to put a boy ahead of a friendship. So I waited until Michelle left the country for a year on a student exchange program when we were eighteen. Michael and I had a fling of sorts but as soon as it became apparent that he was actually interested in me and wasn't a complete prick, I ran a mile. I still regret it. I remember being very upset when I heard about his marriage a few years later, so possibly I had some totally misguided fantasy that we would wind up together in the end – or does everyone just get nostalgic about their first love?

So I blew it with Michael, and I did something similar at university with a couple of guys who were interested and might have pursued me if I'd given them the slightest encouragement. But I didn't. Back then, I put up a lot of defences for a young man to get through and one of them was being funny. I relied very heavily on sarcasm in those post-school years, protecting myself both from being rejected and revealing how scared I was. I have to concede that if someone isn't that confident themselves and the person they're keen on is giving them nothing but barbed one-liners to work with, then they're probably going to retreat pretty quickly.

Here's the thing: when I look back, I can see that some perfectly nice men were attracted to me but I assumed that meant there was something wrong with them. I grew up seeing men treat women badly, so was programmed to accept this. Why would I want to hang out with a guy who might make me feel good about myself when I could keep hurling myself at blokes who weren't remotely interested? It really was a terrific plan!

WHEN I GROW UP, I'LL BE A FEMINIST PRINCESS

Christ, it would be good if you could travel back in time, wouldn't it? One of the questions journalists love to pull out during interviews is 'What do you wish you could have told your younger self?' I wish I could've said to the nineteen-year-old me, 'If a man likes you it doesn't mean he's a psychopath, but if you like him, he probably is.'

I blew another opportunity just before I left Perth. One of my jobs was in a family-run Italian restaurant, Fasta Pasta. It was as sophisticated as the name suggests but the family was lovely, even if some of the young men they employed were questionable. I'll always remember one of the chefs, his fists deep in a bowl of garlic butter, pulling them out, showing them to me and saying, 'Anal, anal, anal.' What a flirt!

He and another chef used to love watching me on the restaurant floor. It took me sometime to realise that this was because when the light caught my blouse at a certain angle it became completely transparent. That might also explain the three-thousand-dollar tip I got, along with an offer of employment at Hooters.

One of the waiters, however (another Andrew), was just adorable. I think he was a cousin of the couple who ran the place and he worked there casually while studying. He was smart, funny and very sweet. We caught the same bus into work and would occasionally go and have cocktails after a shift. Naturally, I assumed he wasn't remotely interested in me. Several years later, after I'd moved to Melbourne, I bumped into him one New Year's Eve in Perth and we wound up sleeping together. The sex was drunken and clumsy but I loved seeing him and remember very fondly the breakfast he made for me the next morning. This was when he told me that if I'd asked him to accompany me to Melbourne when I'd left, he would have. For a comedian, I really do have lousy timing.

I have well and truly outgrown this tendency of ignoring nice men who might be keen on me (although possibly about a decade or two too late) but it did follow me to Melbourne. One of my early jobs was in a cafe, where a guy I was extremely attracted to clearly felt the same way. He came to my house for dinner one night, and when it became obvious that he was too drunk to drive I actually suggested he spend the night in my HOUSEMATE'S BED WITH MY HOUSEMATE IN IT. I mean, can you fucking believe it? 'I really like you, I think you like me. We're both pleasantly drunk so why don't you sleep with my friend?' I hadn't slept with anyone at this point, so the whole idea of being in bed with a man would have been scary, but this guy was kind and – how I hate to say it – that was the real problem.

I've never understood how a person can know intellectually that they're worthwhile but at the same time feel completely worthless. What's up with that? I suppose what's up with it is that the facts don't hold as much sway as the stories we're taught to tell ourselves, and my story meant that I didn't believe I deserved kind treatment. I would keep chasing men like my father and brother for years. I may have only just recently stopped.

I boarded the train to Melbourne and   a second thought. Most of my close friends fr did the same thing, that year or soon after. At tha you wanted a career in the arts, Perth wasn't the Aus lian city to be in. But perhaps it was also true that we all wanted to leave this big country town with its isolation, beaches, perfect weather and wildness. We couldn't wait to get away from our childhoods and our parents. I wouldn't have done anything differently but I do marvel at how little I considered what I was leaving behind. I knew, too, I wouldn't return, other than to visit. I felt like I'd always known it. I can honestly say that at no point in the thirty-odd years since that train trip have I ever thought about living there again.

Melbourne has been my present for a long time now but back then it was my future, and in that future I knew I would be without my family, I would have a successful career and I would meet my prince. I only knew one person in this new city but I understood friendship and its importance, so I wasn't worried about meeting people. I was ambitious and liked hard work, so wasn't really worried on that front either. I also had the ignorance of youth, which enables you to throw yourself into situations because you have no real clue about what you're up against. I still had no idea about men but surely I'd find one in no time, because my god, they were just everywhere!

4
Buggerlugs
My Disastrous History with Men

I arrived in Melbourne the year I turned twenty and had no doubt that, now my life had begun, I would meet Mr Right. While I wasn't interested in getting hitched, I was keen to meet the man I would grow old with. I didn't expect it to be the first guy I slept with. (And just as well it wasn't; he was a very nice drummer but I certainly didn't think, even while being in a Baileys Irish Cream haze, JACKPOT! I'm done looking!) After all, I was a liberated woman, wasn't I, who would probably have sex with *several* men before winding up with a boyfriend. Then, as was the norm, we would move in together.

Really, I only wanted one 'the one', but Niall's girlfriend (she of the life-changing book on feminism) had told me I would probably even fall in love several times during my life, which seemed exciting – it all did! There was something so deliciously terrifying about my feelings of lust, nudity and sex. (Could I sound more Catholic?) It was all so unknown, this path that would lead to discovering my soulmate.

Unfortunately, I was, as I've said, in my twenties, and who knew what was going on in their twenties? I was a mess for that whole decade. But I still blindly got on with looking for that guy I was going to shack up with. And I looked everywhere. It was like I had my boy radar on every time I left the house. Occasionally I may even have checked the freezer and the toilet cistern to see if a foxy young gentleman was just waiting in there for me. I always seemed to have an attraction or a crush on the go. I think I fell for every waiter that served me in this sophisticated new city, along with every Blundstone-and-flannel-shirt-wearing boy with a ute who drank at my local, hopped up on cheap speed.

When I finally started having sex at twenty-one, I think a part of me believed I was a happy, well-adjusted version of Dorothy Parker – simply picking men up for my own amusement in a modern way, never caring if I saw them again but hell-bent on where my next martini and bon mot were coming from. That was how my girlfriends and I would make our encounters sound when we turned them into funny stories for each other, but the truth is that I always hoped each liaison would wind up turning into a relationship (well, maybe not the guy whose idea of a date was taking me to a kebab shop).

I thought each man had at least the possibility of being

my true love, and in the main that's why I slept with them, so I think my heart got a tiny bit cracked every time. Of course, women should sleep with as many people as they want to for whatever reason, but I think what I was doing was waiting to be able to tell the tale that ended with, 'And you know what? I've seen him a few times since that drunken first night and I think we really like each other.' Even the couple of times that did happen, my stories never seemed to end well – but you be the judge.

Actually, before we get to that, let's consider how amazing it is to be an attractive, young, straight white male. It must really rock. The world has always been and for the most part continues to be your oyster. If you choose to, you can have a lot of sex. Many of the men I slept with seemed very comfortable with the idea of putting it about as much as they could. As one of them said to me, 'We're allowed to have fun, aren't we?'

This particular guy had a great deal of fun, with me and many other women. I had fun with him too, for a while, but that stopped when I realised that I was in love and he was simply really digging putting his cock in me and then getting on with his life. (Not with his penis still in me, although I'm sure guys have tried that. 'Sorry baby, I thought I could mow the lawn and still be inside you. Here's your ear.')

Men are very good at compartmentalising when it comes to getting their rocks off. I read stories now about women who sleep with a man they've met on Tinder and spot him swiping right again while they're putting their clothes back on to leave. If that app had existed when I was in my twenties, most of the men I'll be telling you about in this chapter would have done exactly the same.

One of my mistakes was assuming that if a man had sex with me, then he must be at least a little bit interested. In my defence, that film revolving around a young man fucking an apple pie was yet to come out, but even if it had been out I probably would have thought, Sure, it's a little freaky but maybe he has deep feelings for pastry? Maybe he's doing that because one day he wants to marry a flan.

The other problem, as I've already mentioned, was that I wasn't just looking for any old guy to shack up with, I wanted a real partner in crime. I once heard Indigenous writer and performer Steven Oliver say, 'I don't want to fall for someone, I want them to step up to me.' For years I naively believed that most people want to be in a relationship with a like-minded equal, so I often went after guys who seemed like risk-takers, larger than life characters who, I thought, didn't want to marry, have kids or work in an office. Men who wanted to experiment with drugs and ideas and different ways of living!

I'm not saying I wanted to spend my days writing poetry, taking ayahuasca and living in a yurt, although actually, in my twenties that probably would have struck me as pretty appealing. But in my experience, these sorts of men never wind up with their female equivalent. They wind up, like my father, with a woman who will look after them, who will be waiting at home while they go off and have the adventures. They might not want the nine-to-five job but they do want the security of having someone who, after scolding them, will nurse them through their hangovers. It's almost like they delegate; so they don't have to worry about their foibles, they marry someone who'll do it for them.

I didn't know that, though, when I threw myself at painters, actors, writers and even a photographer. I thought these creative men would want nothing better than another inspired soul to live their unusual life with, but I now understand that there was only ever room for one artist and it certainly wasn't me. There are a million reasons why the men you're about to encounter were not interested in having a relationship with yours truly (I do have very pointy elbows for a start) but at the time, I always assumed it was because there was something wrong with me. I don't think that anymore.

I'm going to refer to the men in my tales as 'buggerlugs'. My friend Andrea's mother, the much-loved Nola, used that term for any man who'd treated her daughter a bit shabbily. This could apply to a casual acquaintance or someone Andrea had dated for a while. Nola often knew their name, but if they crossed a certain line she would say things like, 'How's old buggerlugs?' The word is probably too kind for some of the men I'm going to mention, but it's a great word and I don't want to use names (I've even conflated a couple of buggerlugs into one person), because I'm not interested in blaming anyone, I just want to try to understand what the hell was going on with them and me.

To be honest, reflecting on these stories has been no day at the beach but – at the risk of sounding like a literature/language/cultural studies major – by viewing them through the lens of gender, I've come to take it all much less personally and to see everyone involved, including myself, as less of a dipshit.

My first artsy buggerlugs was a very handsome painter that I met at a wedding in Perth a couple of years, and men, after losing my virginity. It ended when I found out I was adopted: after momentarily trying to comfort me, he stuck his hand in my underpants. It's a real shame that he didn't pursue a career in counselling, he definitely had a knack for it. But the world kept giving him positive feedback. When I was with him, women literally followed him around – one slightly older female used to drive him everywhere in the hope that he would eventually fuck her. I should have told her to pretend she was upset so he could have provided some succour with his wang. (Narcissists beware, though: years later I heard that his mother had tried to have him exorcised and that he'd been caught trying to masturbate a horse.)

There was the buggerlugs whose band often shared the bill with me when I was beginning to do stand-up. I had a crush on him and so when we wound up in bed together, I was thrilled. I secretly thought he was way too attractive for me, and couldn't believe it when he hung around the next day and we saw some musicians he knew play at a bar nearby. It didn't seem unreasonable of me the following week to call the number he'd given me. 'Hi,' I said, 'it's

Judith.' 'Oh,' he replied, 'what do you want?' I really should have read between the lines at that point and said, 'Do you deliver pizza?' but instead I asked him out. I was independent, I was sassy, I could ask a guy on a date, couldn't I?

I arrived at the designated pub just in time to see him leave. Of all the gin joints, I'd picked the establishment where his ex-girlfriend was having drinks on her brief return to Australia before she rejoined the guy she'd left him for. This was the reason he gave for leaving when I caught up with him still determined to have dinner (for those of you wondering, this was in the time before mobile phones). Of course I later assumed that he must have been embarrassed to be seen with me – even though he was in a cover band and my career was on the ascent, it would never have occurred to me that I was the one slumming it, not him. I can't remember if I paid for dinner but I certainly bought him a rose when a man came up selling them – I was nowhere near as attractive as his ex-girlfriend but a fun gesture would obviously make him forget that and he'd be dazzled by my independence and spontaneity. Sure, the rose hadn't worked the last time, but this guy wasn't gay, I COULD TURN THIS NIGHT AROUND.

No, I couldn't – the real question is, why was I even trying?

Then, god help me, there were the actors. There was the buggerlugs who, after a fun one-night stand, asked me out for a date. His best friend joined us, which was lucky because buggerlugs spent the entire night talking to everyone else in the bar apart from us. At least when I left, his buddy and I could share a cab. I bumped into buggerlugs months later and he said, 'You were really weird that night.' And he was right; I shouldn't have seemed so put out, I mean, who goes on a date to actually talk to the person they're with? Why should he have wasted his evening talking about his career with just me when he could involve at least a dozen other people?

There was another actor buggerlugs who asked me to leave first thing in the morning because the tape of a soccer final had just been delivered. That's right, a TAPE, so he could have watched it ANYTIME. Years later I bumped into him at a party and his conversation was so self-obsessed that I suddenly became aware of how uncomfortable my shoes were and said, 'I'm in a lot of pain and have to sit down.' Turns out it wasn't the shoes – on my way to a chair I started talking to someone who asked me a question and the ache vanished. (I actually knew a woman who had a rule that if she asked a man three questions in a row and didn't get one back, she walked away. She died an eighty-year-old virgin.)

It's amazing what you can block out when you're attracted to someone. Jan, when she worked as a nurse in a relatively small city, often ran into men she'd been infatuated with years earlier, encounters that only ever left her relieved that they hadn't got together. She often found herself wondering, My god, was he always that boring?

I think another factor with some of these creative buggerlugs was their anxiety about masculinity. They had to make sure their painting or acting didn't make them seem a little *loose-wristed* (as my father liked to say, which I always thought sounded like they had a poorly attached prosthetic hand), so there was definitely some overcompensating going on in terms of drinking, drugs and womanising. I suppose that's where the cliché of the hard-living Hemingway type came from in the first place. I grew to understand that such men don't really want competition in this area (unless it involved watching me have sex with another guy, as one of them suggested).

While I can see this now, I couldn't when I met the writer buggerlugs who flirted with me outrageously but had a girlfriend overseas. The night we met he covered me with glue; it sounds like an Officeworks mishap but it was hot and somewhat illicit. We spent a lot of time together, mainly drinking, but he did also introduce me to heroin, which was thoughtful. We talked about working together. His girlfriend came back, they broke up ... and he asked for my friend Helen's number. They started sleeping together, so the only penetration that came my way was via a syringe. He seemed confused that I wasn't quite as available to him after he'd started fucking my friend. Would I have taken heroin if I hadn't been a bit in love? Of course not. I was convinced we were kindred spirits, but I now suspect, knowing a little about the woman he went on to marry, that he was never going to wind up with a girl who could drink him under the table. He also typified the notion that many of those Hemingwayesque creatives embrace: everything runs second to your art, especially women, unless they're fulfilling the role of muse. We might have wound up together if I'd been less of a pisshead, knew how to play the lyre, and done a lot more wistful staring off into the middle distance.

Writers and artists aside, for many misguided years I thought that the ideal prince would be another stand-up. Who would understand me better than a colleague? How wonderful to be with someone you could work with! Imagine all those hours spent making each other laugh. And that did happen with some comedian buggerlugs, just rarely for more than one evening. I was a chump.

I could have saved myself time by watching any of Judd Apatow's movies or a bunch of other rom-coms: they're all populated by hopeless, funny men who are 'saved' by smart, sensible women. Although when I was in my twenties it was a little different – the queen of the romantic comedy was Meg Ryan. Remember when it seemed like every straight man on the face of the earth wanted to marry her? This was in the *When Harry Met Sally* days, when she looked less like a mop crossed with a duck. It wasn't just that she was beautiful in that girl-next-door way, she was cute and quirky and left all the really funny lines to Billy Crystal. Most men don't want to wind up with a woman who's as funny or funnier than them, whereas ladies love a man with a sense of humour. I've even heard of one particularly unattractive but very talented British comic being sent underwear by a supermodel. Mind you, I have wardrobes full of jocks sent to me by the Hemsworth brothers. I wish they'd leave me alone.

In my late twenties I went to the Montreal Comedy Festival for the first time and met female stand-ups from other countries. I remember how relieved I was to discover that my experience was in fact an international phenomenon: funny women do not have a great success rate with men, comedians or otherwise. I once asked an English comic, my friend Alan Davies, why he thought that was. His theory is that every relationship includes a performer and an audience member. To paraphrase Alan, in a healthy relationship you take turns in those roles, but most men always want to be the performer, with the woman applauding their efforts.

I wonder if it has something to do with the old line that men are afraid women will laugh at them, while women are afraid that men will kill them. I saw a variant of this in respect to online dating: women are afraid that a strange man will kill them, while men are afraid of going on a date with someone fat. (Now, that *would* be terrifying. Forget films like *Jaws* and *Rogue*, why has no one ever made *Love Handles*?) The takeaway is: men want us to laugh at their jokes and be thin, and women want to not be murdered.

The wonderful Denise Scott, who was smart enough to meet her partner BEFORE she became a stand-up, thinks it also has something to do with the fact that women are supposedly meant to be mysterious. It's certainly true that if you date a funny lady, you're not going to be left wondering about too many aspects of her life. In fact, you'll probably hear her talk about her sex life, her bodily functions and a whole host of things that most people go out of their way to keep to themselves but which we choose to share with strangers. So *now* you tell me that routine about a woman injecting warm oil into my anus to cure my irritable bowel syndrome wasn't attractive? Who knew?

Naturally it did not work out with any of the comedians I fell for. How did I ever think those men might have wanted to share the laughter when they were usually surrounded by women who were only too happy to buy a ticket for the front row of their bedroom? Boy, I wish I could take back some of the time I wasted on a couple of these comedian buggerlugs. Like the one I fell for in my late twenties who, when I returned from the Edinburgh Fringe Festival, announced that he was now sleeping with many women and that we would have to make dates so he could squeeze me in (as opposed to living with me, as he virtually had been before I left).

He had a number of the masculine traits I seemed to find so appealing; he was a big smoker and drinker, but I don't think he'd ever got over the fact that he wasn't something blokier, such as a butcher who slaughtered cows with his teeth. The comedy stuff always seemed to vaguely embarrass him, so he often acted like he'd done no work at all on his material, lest it appear he actually cared about his writing or joke structure. Yet his talent was another reason I was attracted to him, and I put up with his philandering, thinking it might be the price for being with such an unusual and quite brilliant man.

Not long after returning from Scotland I took him to see a band I knew he would love. We went backstage and then on to a friend's pub where we were made a bit of a fuss of. What I was desperately trying to say was, Look at me, look at me; see, other people like me, this could be our life, I'm doing all this for you. Unfortunately, he seemed to be thinking, Who is this chick who seems to think she deserves equal billing in my movie? I don't think it was an accident that at the end of our supposed date, he told me he had to go and fuck another woman to prove he could maintain an erection with her.

A lot of women want a prince who's more than just some hot guy who's great in the sack, but I think that's all some men want in a woman. It took me a long time to see that was the case for this particular buggerlugs because I was in love with him and he kept sleeping with me, so despite his behaviour I kept clutching onto that very weak straw. Some time later, another lady who'd had similar feelings for him at one point said to me, 'Jude, I spent years thinking that there was so much more to him and then I realised that there was just so much less.' We had this conversation in the DVD section of JB Hi-Fi and I'll never forget walking out of the store and literally feeling the penny dropping inside me.

I was never very good at sleeping with people just for the sake of it but I did give it a crack with one buggerlugs when I was in my twenties. We're friends now but back then I don't think we even liked each other. I mention him because years later, when he was married with children, he'd drunkenly text me late at night saying that we should 'catch up', or that I was 'special' or a 'great girl'. In his case, I think it was completely innocent but there have been cases where a bloke clearly wanted more than a catch-up. Most recently a buggerlugs simply texted, 'Hey you x,' and followed up with a drunken message. I later told a mutual acquaintance, who replied, 'So you know he got married again a couple of days after that?' I didn't. I wonder how many other women he texted that night? Of course I was flattered, I'm sure I was the only lady he contacted from his list of people whose surname started with the letter L.

Still, I wish I could say that I'd never slept with a married man, but it seems that the things single men find threatening are exactly what some married men are after! And although I'm not at all trying to excuse my behaviour, I've not always been wise – or sober – enough to get out of the way. Plus, it pains me to report, I was grateful for the interest. The bottom line is that ninety-nine per cent of the time, if a man I knew and liked made a pass at me, I couldn't get my G-string off fast enough (I hasten to add that the only time I've been near a G-string was when I learnt the guitar).

One of the married buggerlugs was the man who told me he'd left his wife when he hadn't. Ironically, before he actually made a move, the thing I liked about him was that he appeared to be a devoted husband and father. When he was with me it became apparent that while he might not always have gone to the effort of pretending to leave his wife for other people, he'd certainly fucked around on her plenty. Why didn't my alarm bells go off? Because you think it's going to be different with you. I honestly think I have some special kind of deafness which has prevented me from hearing alarms so many times that it's just as well I'm not a firefighter. I think I've literally been on fire and thought, It sure is warm in here but how lucky I am not to be in any danger! as I poured some more petrol on myself and asked whichever bounder I was with, 'Please, light my cigarette.'

There was the Scottish buggerlugs I spent a year with, him screwed up by the fact that his parents and one of his brothers were dead before he was twenty-five, me by having just found out I was adopted. No one else would have us, so we clung to each other for a while, but ultimately had more 'thank god that's over' sex in the days following the break-up than we'd had in months, so his parting gifts to me were cystitis and a yeast infection. (Ah memories, pity you can't put thrush in a photo album.)

Then there was the ex-speed-addict buggerlugs I wound up with instead of the single, attractive and very eligible actor my friend was trying to set me up with. The most that could be said for him was he was breathing and interested. Still, better that than the actor, who I've run into since and who turns out to be one of my favourite breed of men, the sort that, if they don't want to fuck you, literally don't see you.

Eventually, all of this started to take more of a toll on me than I realised. I had the best sex of my life with a buggerlugs acrobat. I then had sex with a buggerlugs who looked a lot like that acrobat. Except that, I didn't – he came back to my place, we kissed, and apparently I repeatedly called him an arsehole and he left. I can't even say that this was in my twenties. It was alarming; I've never been one of those drunks who turns into a different person. I get horribly repetitive and pass out – but that's intriguing, isn't it? I don't quite know what was going on in my brain that evening but I suspect I was very angry with someone, if not necessarily him. Although maybe I was a bit psychic. Mortified, I offered to take him out for a drink, no strings attached, to make up for it. He said he'd pass on the drink but did I think I could help him get his documentary funded?

To the best of my knowledge that's the only time I've behaved like that in the boudoir, but there have been a couple of other occasions when I've drunkenly ranted at a man about someone else. It feels like I've repressed so much emotion when it comes to the opposite sex that now and then it's bubbled out with the wrong person. My only saving grace is that I'm completely unintelligible by that stage, and my companion is always in a similar state, so it's possible they're doing their own insane babbling to a drink coaster. I never recall any of it – I only ever know about it because, after telling me about their hangover and cracked rib, my drinking partner will say, 'Yeah you seemed really angry about something but I don't know what.'

I probably didn't either. It's a very weird feeling to discover that you *were* angry about something and didn't quite know it. So many of the times that I'd chalked up to something lacking in me, or to misunderstandings or the crappiness of an individual buggerlugs, now seem to me less a series of shitty incidents and more a structural problem. And not just with me. It's taken me years to zoom out and finally see the bigger picture. Mind you, we've only recently looked back at the sixties and understood that it wasn't quite the same swinging, psychedelic paradise for the ladies that it was for the men.

The pill had changed the world by then but feminism was yet to really hit, and I don't doubt that a lot of women felt they had to put out or be seen as 'uptight, man'. The free love was a lot freer for the men. I may not have been going to San Francisco with a flower in my hair but my notion that I was independent and liberated suited the guys I slept with very well. They weren't thinking, What a bold, free-thinking lady! They were thinking, Great, she puts out.

I was aware that most of my friends were winding up in relationships and I just assumed that if I kept getting drunk and sleeping with fuckwits, then obviously I would too. What? It never seemed to occur to me that I could do better, or that sleeping with virtually any likeable rogue who would have me wasn't panning out. And it took me even longer to identify another aspect to the imbalance in my relationships: money.

It was very rare that I didn't pay for the good times, and I don't just mean emotionally. For example, there was the buggerlugs I went up to and said, 'Do you want to fuck me?'

It turns out that really does work! But I wasn't taking any chances. We left the venue we were at, went to a late-night bar and restaurant where I paid for everything. We had breakfast the next morning and I'm pretty sure I paid for that too. I told myself I was doing it because I was generous and he was poor, but the truth is that I was overcompensating – I didn't think I was enough. What I didn't understand was that often when I took out my wallet, I may as well have said, 'I'll get this because you're obviously not man enough to.'

I'm not sure that men even realise how primal the urge is to be the main breadwinner, but it makes sense: if you hold the financial strings, you have the power. It's one of the reasons I vowed to never be dependent on anyone else's wages, having heard my parents argue about money so often. I never, ever wanted to be in a situation where I had to ask someone to pay for me. I know I'm lucky – it's not fair that women over fifty are the group now most likely to be homeless, thanks to sacrifices made in child rearing. Their careers and superannuation benefits were stalled while they did the unpaid and vital work of parenting.

Men may feel that they should be the top earner in a partnership yet that doesn't always stop them from taking money when it's offered – they just seem to hate themselves for doing it and resent the person who's extending the offer. When I had a very well paid job on commercial radio, the gentleman I was with seemed very happy to live off me although I now think that it bothered him a great deal. I can't stress enough that he's a decent man who I loved. He's an artist and I'd told him to take six months off his bill-paying job to concentrate on his creativity. Unfortunately, that turned into two years. (At one point Jan told him to get a job. I was mortified but secretly delighted. It made no difference.) Now I can't quite believe that, apart from driving me around occasionally, he didn't feel the need to do anything (he didn't cook or clean) except mooch about in his beautiful studio overlooking the ocean while I was having my soul destroyed working in a dreadful job for which I would have a lot more to show if he hadn't so cheerfully spent my money.

We had a joint bank account (something I'll never do again; nor will I ever share my passwords, but more on that later) and he would delight in paying for expensive meals for my friends, sometimes even buying them presents. When it ended, I was the one who moved into a hotel, despite the fact that I'd bought the house we lived in (I then paid the rent for it after it was sold because I couldn't afford the mortgage repayments anymore). One friend said to me that each dollar he took from the sale would be one less increment that I respected him. But that didn't stop him from taking half of the money. Couples come to all sorts of arrangements about finances of course, and if you're doing the majority of the unpaid work that keeps a household running then it's entirely different. Lovely as this man is, he was not raising our children, he was being one.

Although to the best of my knowledge he didn't behave like this before and hasn't since, I'm confident that I'm the only partner who earned substantially more than he did and I wonder if that was the issue. Was his passivity a kind of punishment? Not consciously perhaps, but being with me wouldn't have done a lot for his ego and maybe that explains some of his behaviour.

And while he certainly knew I thought he should get a job, it never occurred to me to raise the issue of his contributing in any other way. I was grateful to have someone. He'd moved cities to be with me, we were going to be together forever so I'd get my turn, wouldn't I? But despite convincing myself of this, I knew I'd never be able to let someone else provide for me without giving something in return. Blow jobs at the very least. I've come to understand that my earning a lot of money wasn't the only reason I paid all the bills during this period – the bigger reason was my somehow feeling I needed to. It'd become a habit of mine, not just because I'm bad with finances and I hate stinginess; I thought I could make up for my perceived shortcomings by paying. Even when I'd landed the part of girlfriend or lover, I acted like I was still auditioning. I never stopped feeling like I was the lucky one, that I didn't deserve this, so I'd better cover all the bases to try to lock this shit down.

There was another reason, too, that I liked getting my wallet out and that was booze.

The mother of one of the buggerlugs told me I drank like a man and I think that was definitely one of my downfalls. I drank because I liked it and because it helped me relax in situations where I was massively uncomfortable, but also, I now recognise, because I was emulating my father. The part of the jigsaw that I didn't see back then is that society rewards, or certainly doesn't condemn, men for that behaviour but it never applauds women for doing the same. At the time, I took the comment about my masculine drinking as a compliment! Whereas in fact, this older woman was calling me a drunken slut who she almost certainly didn't want her son to have anything to do with.

The reality is that we women aren't just frowned upon for getting drunk, we're considered by our culture to be 'asking for it'. A buggerlugs – no, that's too kind a word, a bastard – I knew and liked wound up trying to fuck me in the front seat of his car without a condom. I was out of it enough to have no memory of how I ended up with him inside me but I did have the presence of mind to tell him to stop, which he did. I suggested we go back to his place or mine and use a condom. That would have made the whole thing much less rapey, which would've been great. He declined that offer, announced that he had a girlfriend and dropped me in the middle of nowhere at three am. As I said in a subsequent routine, 'He didn't just slow down, he actually stopped the car. Christ, he was a keeper.'

I finally found a cab, took my ripped tights and dignity home, and passed out in front of the heater and burned myself. Incredibly, when I bumped into this guy a few months later he was furious with me. This was because I'd confided to some mutual friends (who turned out to be not so mutual) that the whole thing had left me feeling appalling. I felt sick when I saw him. He made a disparaging comment that made it clear he hated me: I was obviously just meant to keep my feelings to myself and not have the gall to paint him in a bad light to his mates.

I've asked myself, Well, was that assault? I certainly don't remember consenting but I don't remember a lot of the evening. What is certain is that he's older than me and knew exactly what he was doing. At the very least I was taken advantage of by a complete prick.

Even more mystifying, though, is that when I saw him many years later at an opening, I went out of my way to be civil to him. I knew this was because I just wanted to 'make everything okay'. It wasn't okay. I've already spoken about repressing my anger – that's bad enough – but how did I wind up being the person who tried to make things better when *I'd* been fucked over? Was it because I'd spent years doing that with my brother and father, or are women just hardwired to make men feel better even if we're the wronged party? I'm happier when everyone just gets along – but everyone doesn't just get along, so what happens then? Unconsciously I've bought into the idea of it being their world, in which I'd better not cause any trouble or make a fuss. So, if an evening went south, I would put it down to me.

When I was newly arrived in Melbourne, one of my bosses (who was twenty years older than me) relished telling me stories that involved him getting erections or being in the change room while his girlfriend tried on lingerie. I'd naively confided in him that I was a virgin and he loved talking about that too. Being paid this weird kind of attention by a much older man, who also thought I was funny, was new to me and I actually began to find him attractive. My god, *did* I? Was I flattered by his harassment? I threw myself at him one night and he recoiled in horror, pretending that all his attention had been imagined by me. I was so innocent I didn't understand that what he was really appalled by was probably not me but seeing the results of his own behaviour. Who am I kidding? He was just a louse.

These are all incidents I've re-examined in light of the #MeToo movement. We've all got stories, haven't we? Some of the nicest men I know, including gay men, have grappled with #MeToo and when they have I've often heard the phrase 'witch hunt' come out of their mouths. Some men think that women shouldn't put themselves in certain situations – so it's us who are at fault, not the culture. When even the men I consider decent are still blaming us to some degree, it's very difficult not to feel disheartened. Perhaps when the world is run by you and for you, it's hard to see that the problem is with that same world.

One of the men I talked to about all this – and I welcomed the fact that he wanted to have the discussion – told me that many years ago he'd yelled something out at a woman at a bus stop. Nothing offensive, but he'd been surprised by his need to shout something out of a car window. He's a thoughtful person and so questioned why he'd done it and came to the conclusion: because he could.

When it comes to car abuse, my two favourite lines among those that have been yelled at me are 'Why don't you raise your skirt a bit higher and show us your crack you slut?' and 'I wouldn't fuck you with a dead dog's dick.' I mean, you've got to admire the alliteration in that last one, he'd really put some thought into it. To be fair, it was my fault – I had been walking up to men in cars and asking them if they'd copulate with me using a deceased animal's genitals, so he was just giving me a candid response. WHAT IS GOING ON IN THESE MEN'S MINDS?

Maybe, as my paper-holding comedian suggested onstage, the answer is: nothing. It's simply their world, their movie and they can do whatever they like. We are just these other creatures who they become more or less interested in depending on what they need or want at any given moment.

I was on a packed tram not long ago when a very inebriated man sat next to a young woman and clearly terrified her with his aggressive advances. I was sitting opposite and desperately wanted to defuse the situation but had no idea how, not least because I was equally intimidated. Thankfully, a lovely guy stood next to him and completely disarmed him by engaging him in conversation. The whole tram audibly exhaled when this drunk jerk got off a few stops later. I was furious at how his presence had put us all on edge, especially the women.

The good news for me, of course, was that he would never have sat next to this old crone. No one wanks or yells at me anymore, because men don't see me, a phenomenon I had cause to think about recently at the theatre, of all places. I saw a smart, entertaining show that involved three women sharing snippets of real-life conversations they'd had over twenty years. Naturally it covered relationships, babies, break-ups and, now, perimenopause. I loved it. It's so rare to see a piece of art that's about women just being. But the one interlude that horrified me was when they spoke of the male gaze (where a woman is objectified for the sake of heterosexual male pleasure). Hey, I studied film theory when I was at university. I know who feminist film theorist Laura Mulvey is but I hadn't thought about all that in years. I'd never admitted to myself how much I'd internalised that gaze. It wasn't just something I recognised in movies, it was often how I saw myself, and I frequently imagined that a man was watching me. Never a particular man, just some anonymous male presence.

Mostly, I thought about a guy observing me when I was doing mundane chores like washing the dishes, but sometimes when I was doing yoga. Turns out, I'm not doing yoga for any kind of spiritual awakening – I just want some bloke to think I'm a flexible babe. Sure, the gaze is about wanting to be desired but it's also about relegating our experience to the sidelines, being the other, living in a place that is run by men where we feel like the interlopers.

I recently sat on a panel where we discussed the movie *Thelma and Louise*. Naturally, we had to unpack the ending where the two women drive off a cliff. Both characters had 'crossed over' and couldn't go back to living in a patriarchal world. A world where they were harassed, patronised, abused and raped. How else could the film have ended? If they wanted to escape that world, where else could they have gone?

No wonder I was trying to behave like Dad. Who wouldn't want to be the one doing the gazing, the one people had to please? I'm certainly not the only woman, particularly of my generation, who thought that behaving like a man was the answer. What a pity I/we didn't ask ourselves what we wanted our lives to be like as women. We only knew what we didn't want and that was our mothers' lives.

We're the generation who really suffered from thinking we could have it all. I didn't want children, so the definition of 'all' in my case was having a man and being able to act like one, but the reality is that women are punished for that. Men seem to have the prerogative even down to fucking us. Isn't it interesting that there isn't a female equivalent for the word 'incel'? The involuntary male celibate who doesn't have much luck with the ladies but who doesn't blame himself, he blames us. In fact these men hate us because their presumption is that sex is their right and we're depriving them of it.

I knew none of this in my twenties of course, I just kept stitching my heart back together, pouring another drink and forging on, genuinely believing that it would work out next time. I could have saved myself a lot of time if I'd simply listened to Stevie Nicks. Like every woman with a beating heart, I'm a fan of Ms Nicks, but never more so than when I read a recent interview with her where she said, 'People would say to me: "It would be very hard to be Mr Stevie Nicks." And I'm going: well, yeah, probably unless you were just a really nice guy that was really confident in himself, not jealous of me, liked my friends, enjoyed my crazy life and had fun with it. And, of course, there are very few men like that. I'm an independent woman and am able to take care of myself, and that is not attractive to a man.'

Which reminds me that there's a story I haven't told: one of the buggerlugs I was in love with said to me, when I mentioned that I would miss him when I went to perform at the Edinburgh Fringe, 'Well, you don't have to go.' I realised that this hadn't occurred to me, and now that it had I had no intention of not pursing my goal of doing a season at one of the world's top comedy festivals.

Not chasing my ambitions was never an option for me. I was never prepared to put my career on hold or sacrifice an opportunity for a man. I genuinely wanted to share my life with someone and believed at the time that it was my priority, but the kind of guy I was attracted to was never going to take a back seat to me, or what I really wanted, sit beside me. So it turns out Mr Right was never as important as what I did for a living. I'm going to quote Stevie again: 'It's not my job, it's who I am.'

5

Genius
Comedy is My Life

I hated Hannah Gadsby's show *Nanette*.

I didn't share this fact with many people because at the time it felt tantamount to throwing my arms in the air and saying, 'Hey everyone, isn't it about time we just all gave Woody Allen a break?' I hasten to add that I'm not only a big fan of Hannah's work but like to think of her as a friend, so my secret opinion put me in quite a pickle.

The problem was that I took the show personally; I was angered by her denouncement of self-effacing comedy because that's what I've always done, put myself down onstage. Some comedians play high-status as compared to their audience but I've never been one of them. I don't have any trouble telling embarrassing stories about my childhood or my dating life (you're nearly a hundred pages in, so I think you're probably across that by now) or simply looking ridiculous by wearing a nude suit or a scuba-diving outfit as part of a show. I'll do pretty much anything for a laugh and I've never let my dignity get in the way of that, so I was also one of those people who thought *Nanette* simply didn't have enough jokes. I've always prided myself on my gag ratio and I believe that when it comes to stand-up comedy there should be punchlines and lots of them. I thought Hannah's show was extremely well written and powerful, but when I read articles about it changing comedy forever I was offended. What did that say about the last thirty years of my career? I'd struggled with and questioned my job but it was enormously important to me – it's the most defining aspect of my life. It was all very well to get angry at men onstage like Hannah did, but try starting out in comedy when it was almost only men performing onstage and I'll tell you about anger.

Do I think I would have had an easier time being a stand-up comedian if I'd had a penis? The answer is YES. Absolutely. This is a question all female comics have been asked a million times and yet it remains difficult to answer publicly without either lying or sounding like you're complaining. I'm not comparing myself to someone running for the Democratic nomination for the President of the US, but when Elizabeth Warren left the race my heart went out to her. She was asked if her gender had been an issue and she replied that this question was a trap for women: 'If I say, "Yeah, there was sexism", everybody says, "Whiner!" If I say, "There was no sexism", about a bazillion women think, "What planet are you from?"'

Her comments ring true for any woman working in an industry where she's in the minority. Of course it's an issue, but we gain little, if anything, by saying so because the real point is that it's not just our careers that would be different if we were men, but our lives. (We'd be spending a lot more time in urinals and, if my father was anything to go by, picking wax out of our ears with a pencil.) About ten years ago, I told some of my industry horror stories to a young female filmmaker and she thought there might be a documentary in it. But when she asked me how many women I thought would talk about this stuff on camera I had to answer that I thought very few would, including me, and I was in a better position than most. I think that documentary could be made now.

When I began, the idea that women weren't funny was all-pervasive; most of the male stand-ups thought that and so did the audiences. Yet I just knew this wasn't true. Some of the funniest people in my life were women. If comedy and tragedy are two sides of the same coin, didn't it make sense that any group who'd been discriminated against would have quite a few lemons to turn into lemonade? Don't most people try to cope with grief and anger by making light of it at times? Don't we crack jokes at wakes? And how can women not be funny when you consider all the shit our bodies put us through? Why did the chicken cross the road? Because of her prolapsed uterus!

In 2018 I was performing in the Spiegeltent in Hobart when one of the crew told me that she had a 'hilarious' story for me. In the middle of my soundcheck, an older man had wandered in and said, 'Oh my god, is that Judith Lucy?' She said, 'Yes,' and he said, 'I despise her and everything she stands for.' I'm a little psychic and I have a feeling, reading between the lines and using all my intuition, that he may not have been a fan. Strangely, I didn't find that story hilarious. The woman, who was much younger than me, asked, 'I don't get it, are you controversial?' I didn't know how to explain that for a long time a female just getting onstage and saying what she thought was very controversial. Only recently I was asked, while on a panel about women in comedy, why some men are still threatened by lady comics and I said, 'Because we take up space.'

When I started out, it felt like we were allowed to take up only a couple of centimetres. It was bad enough onstage but I think the hostility off it was far worse. Some men simply ignored me for years, but I now wonder if that was actually better than when I was 'accepted' and would have to keep my mouth shut when offensive jokes were told or other female comics were slammed for not being as good as the men. To be fair, there were only a handful of men who were truly awful, such as the gentleman who used to tell shockingly homophobic 'jokes' that were completely offensive. He spotted another young female comic standing near me at the back of the room one night while he was performing, pointed her out and said (brace yourself, what's coming is pure Oscar Wilde), 'What's your problem, you cunt?' After that I obviously saw the humour in what he was saying and begged him to write some material for me.

I'll always remember one of the first meetings I had with the D-Generation when I was asked to join the cast of *The Late Show* on the ABC. I was twenty-four and had been doing comedy for about three years. The only other female in the group, Jane Kennedy, wasn't there for some reason and at lunchtime we all walked down the street to pick up a sandwich, me and six men. I remember feeling like I was in a Western. I was young and anxious about my new job but these guys wanted me there, so for once I wasn't trying to make myself invisible in their company. I was struck by how intoxicating it was to be surrounded by men who weren't excluding me. I suddenly understood how some ladies are willing to be 'one of the boys' at the expense of their own sex. I'm glad I can remember that day because, while there were absolutely other men who supported me when I started, it's not a feeling I've had very often. The feeling of inclusion, not the Western bit. I often feel like I'm in the Wild West because I run a brothel and generally only get around in a skirt and corset. It's a great life apart from the tobacco spit on my floor and the syphilis.

It actually took me a long time to realise I was good at my job and I still feel uncomfortable typing that. For years I thought I might be funny but that I could never really be as funny as some of the men. A long time ago, I heard a male comic say to a TV executive about me, 'No you wouldn't want her on the show, she's really rude.' At that point my best routine was about the lines men yelled at me from car windows, so weirdly, if I *was* being obscene, it was simply because I was repeating offensive things men had shouted in order to ruin my day. I may also have had a hilarious routine about a man wanking while I was in a laundromat (this happened) and me wondering if he'd just been a little confused and meant to ask me for some bleach. At the time, though, I just took that male comic's comment as another indication that what I was doing was somehow lesser.

I got laughs in the early years but I always felt like I was an imposter of sorts. I wasn't talking about politics, I wasn't improvising, I was just too . . . me. I worked hard as well, and that didn't seem very cool. I think this has now changed but when I began it seemed like if you hadn't just pulled a syringe out of your arm or a bong from your mouth before you got onstage, with no prepared material, you were trying too hard. Never mind that what was important seemed to be the sheer length of the gig – over two hours in some cases – and impressing the other comedians in the room, rather than the audience's enjoyment.

One man used to love performing in such a way that he would lose the crowd in order to win them back. It was a dangerous game: one night, when he'd just gone on too long and was way too drunk to be even remotely entertaining, he threw himself off the front of the stage. I heard that if his agent and several others who worked for his management company hadn't been there, the audience would have let him fall to the ground. All stand-ups are competitive to some degree but I never understood how the length of someone's spot was such a point of pride. I mean, come on guys, it's not how long it is, it's what you do with it.

Life certainly improved when I resolved to run my own race and not count on comedy to provide me with friends or a social life. (Regrettably it took me a lot longer to realise that I should stop letting it provide me with sex. I shat on my own back doorstep so many times it was like I'd replaced my veranda with a toilet.) I do have some good friends in comedy now but mostly they're women, because several of the men I was close to had a tendency to always put themselves first. I really do need to say, again, that I've had incredible support from various guys in my career but I've also been let down a good number of times.

I've given work to men only to have them not turn up or be lazy to the point of inertia; I've also seen jobs that were promised to me by blokes given to someone else with no explanation. And while I was dying a slow death on breakfast radio some men, who I thought I was close to, flatly refused to come on the show because they obviously thought my failure was contagious.

I used to be very ambitious when it came to my career but I don't believe I've ever put a job or money before a friendship, and that favour hasn't always been returned. Then again, I think some men just reckon relationships should automatically take a back seat when it comes to work and making a living, and that it's all part of the rough-and-tumble of the industry. Whenever I was disappointed in this way, I largely kept it to myself. I can't tell you what a revelation it was when I recently read that women, because we're so programmed not to get angry, often cry instead. It's a fact: most of my tears about my job have been tears of rage.

I will add that this has, mostly, not been my experience with men younger than me. I would like to say that this means all straight, younger male comics deliver enlightened feminist jokes, but some of the material I've heard would indicate that's not the case, especially when it comes to the enduring fascination with the penis. It really is like every male comic thinks they've discovered it for the first time. I've heard sixteen-year-olds, doing their first gig, discuss it and I will never forget seeing Louis CK bang on and on about his semen at the Opera House for what felt like hours. This was when we were all still meant to think he was hilarious and woke. My companion put it very nicely when he turned to me at the end of the gig and said, 'Wow that was a bit of a jizz fest.' I went on to talk about this in my next show and asked the audience, 'So you guys don't mind if I just talk about discharge for twenty minutes, do you?'

What I find doubly galling is that if a woman refers to her vagina, that's apparently all we ever talk about. Like most lady stand-ups I've got one, so I talk about it, but I talk about many other things as well: my vulva, my clitoris, my labia . . . I probably couldn't get over two hours of improvised material out of it, but then again I'm no genius.

I'm not the first woman to point this out but it's such a shame that there are hardly any female geniuses in comedy – or just anywhere – isn't it? The law of averages would suggest that there must be a couple *somewhere*, but apparently only men ever reach those heady heights. The word is generally overused but one of the many reasons I think it's seldom, if ever, bestowed on women in my world is because our material tends to be personal and domestic. Talking about your family, relationship or body is somehow thought of as less creatively exciting than, say, a routine about a kilt made out of yogurt. Making comedy out of experiences many people have had is seen as less impressive than inventing a joke about a salami birdbath, and yet it takes a lot of skill to make the ordinary funny.

I'm aware, incidentally, of how fortunate I am. I've been in this industry and towards the top of it for a very long time now. My manager, Kev, is a glorious kook and I don't think it would even occur to him that a woman couldn't be as funny as a man. Not only have I had his support, but almost without exception I've found the women in comedy magnificent, and the support of my friends has been unfailing. As, of course, has been that of my audiences, who are largely females and gay men.

While I never let the makeup of my crowd colour my choice of material (not consciously anyway), I think I still craved straight male affirmation in the past. God knows why – maybe because I wasn't getting it in my personal life. To be fair, I wanted to appeal to as many people as possible – it's all money in the bank. But as in romance, I like a challenge! And stand-ups always concentrate on the face of the audience member who isn't laughing, so I was fixated on the one demographic that didn't want a bar of me.

I can't tell you how often I've looked out at those watching me perform and seen men sitting there with crossed arms, scowling – hating me! – while their wife or girlfriend, who clearly bought the tickets, laughed in all the right places. I've often wanted to stop the show and say, 'Gary, why don't you unfold your arms, put your legs back together so I can't see the outline of your package, and then just go and get hammered in the bar for the rest of the gig?'

A friend once told me about a young group of men and women who attended one of my shows. The girls laughed from start to finish, but when they were all walking out and their boyfriends declared that I was terrible they all sheepishly agreed. A much more depressing example was a shocking gig in a country town many years ago where I died a terrible death. At the end of the evening, a woman who'd been sitting at a table of all ladies came up to me and said, 'I don't know if you know but we've got the highest rate of sexual assault in the country. I just wanted to say that we all enjoyed the show but we were too afraid to laugh out loud.' Even as I type this I can't believe that actually happened and not very long ago.

There've been exceptions of course. I'll always remember the night two very straight brothers in their late teens were in my front row. I joked that they'd made a terrible mistake and must have thought they were buying tickets to see Tommy Little or that I was a lap dancer, but they assured me they were fans. However I do have actual proof of my lack of straight-male appeal. I was told one of the television networks had tested me with various audience groups and the one bunch who universally loathed me was straight men my age and older. Isn't that lucky? I've now reached a point where men don't even have to meet me to reject me!

This would explain why I can't get a TV show on that network, while men roughly my age and older are given not just one series but sometimes two. I like and admire some of these men but I think it's appalling that there isn't one older female stand-up on this station, and we have some of the finest in the world, in my humble opinion. It's a neat trick that when a woman finally earns the respect she's worked so hard for, in a lot of industries ageism then catches up.

The path is never straightforward either. It's said that, career-wise, men tend to go from point A to point B in a straight line, hopefully towards success, whereas a woman's trajectory looks more like a drunken bee's, going forward then backwards and then around in circles until she eventually makes it onto a stamen, ideally somewhere near the one she was aiming for.

In practical terms, this often means having to make your own career path and, in my world, create your own work. You often have to operate outside TV and radio, especially as you get older, and write books or do podcasts, and thank god there's always live work. It's not that the audiences aren't there, it's just that you have to keep finding different routes to them that bypass the straight white middle-aged men who can't see your value.

Thankfully people are much more aware of the need for diversity now, but even so I'm yet to turn to someone and say, 'Wow, we need to see more forty-plus-year-old white guys on telly. They have really been shafted.' I don't care what those gatekeepers think of me anymore, but it took a long time for me to become indifferent to it.

As for the idea that the affirmation I was chasing was a throwback to the men I grew up with, I know Niall was proud of me but that involved a fair bit of reading between the lines on my part. Mum and Dad rarely saw me live because the main performance was always on at their house, between them, but Mum would gush when she did see things and she kept clippings, while Dad certainly liked that I was on TV. Although it's hard to ignore the fact that he disowned me via a fax right before I went onstage. He knew it would fuck me up. And it did.

Somehow, I managed to convince myself that I should just tough out the panic attacks that followed. They eventually receded, mainly thanks to meditation and better understanding how my mind works but I never thought to go to a doctor and say, 'From the moment I get out of bed in the morning I'm terrified about what's going to happen onstage and it's completely debilitating. I claw my way through the day and then get completely off my face every night as a reward, relieved that I've made it through another show. Do you think I might need some help?'

I was in therapy during some of the worst bouts and yet I DIDN'T MENTION THEM. Why would I? I was fine. I cannot believe that someone like me, who's such a big believer in counselling, somehow thought these attacks were weak and that I should just suck them up and hope that they would eventually go away. It's not lost on me that this is exactly how my father and brother would've approached the situation.

I did some very nutty things to try to stop those attacks. I even remember a period where I would stand in front of the hotel mirror and sing (wait for it) 'I am Woman' as a way of willing myself out of them. It worked! Who needs to see a shrink when you can pretend to be Helen Reddy? (As well as being empowering, maybe I thought lyrics like 'I'm still an embryo with a long, long way to go' might distract me. It's surely the only tune that's ever used the word 'embryo'. I'm disappointed she didn't find a rhyme for 'cervix' or 'fallopian tube'.)

I was completely out of my mind and spending way too much time on my own in hotel rooms, which is never a good thing. I honestly thought I could just clench my teeth and get over it. All this did was make me think about the attacks even more, reinforcing the loop in my brain and ensuring the pattern, and fear, would continue.

For many years that anxiety obliterated the fact that I genuinely love getting up and showing off in front of other people. I sometimes wonder if I was subconsciously punishing myself, not just for my estrangement from my father but also because I was successful. A female pilot once told me that among her colleagues the rate of women in abusive relationships was very high, because a part of them didn't think they deserved to be where they are.

I was on a panel about women in comedy recently where the only female who wasn't apologetic about her success was a younger transwoman. The rest of us wore our accomplishments with embarrassment and stopped just short of saying, Sorry for being good at what we do. When young women who were interested in a career in comedy would ask me for advice, I used to offer the only thing I knew and had tried to do myself: work hard and sell a lot of tickets. I would also 'jokingly' add that they should never expect to get a boyfriend out of it, or for it to do much for their self-esteem. What a mentor! I'm surprised I didn't add, But if you're looking for a job that gives you cirrhosis of the liver, you've come to the right place!

I wonder what I was getting out of it (apart from the cirrhosis). I made money, and now that the attacks have abated, I can say that I largely enjoy it but I've been pretty hard on myself. One of the other reasons anxiety has been such an issue is that, in an effort to be as good if not better than a lot of the men, I've held myself to extremely exacting standards. The general attitude was often that if Mike isn't funny then Mike just isn't a very good stand-up, but if Sally isn't funny, women aren't funny. I never wanted to let myself or the team down. It pains me to say that to this day I'm still way more critical of female performers, for the same reason. It's also why I always try to put as many jokes as possible into my shows – *panic* – some of them will work, won't they? I may be in a man's world but I can be as funny as them, see?

I recently heard an interview with one of the many women whose names we don't remember but whose work has been significant. This woman was instrumental in getting films made during that halcyon period of American independent cinema in the seventies. (Obviously I'd tell you who she is but I just couldn't be bothered looking the chick up. Alright then, it was director/casting director Nessa Hyams). The host spoke about how Nessa and production designer, producer and screenwriter Polly Platt, who is infuriatingly best known for being director Peter Bogdanovich's jilted wife, weren't feminists because: 'They didn't want to rock the boat, they wanted to be in the boat.' I may have been a feminist but I wanted that too.

What a waste of time. They were never going to let those women board. I don't know if comedians can ever really be cool, but I was certainly never going to be one of those guys who smoked onstage and did material that either railed against the world or was opaque with surrealism. A friend told me that a woman at a party once asked her how I could degrade myself the way I did when I performed. (And I'd thought talking about throwing up into my gusset was funny . . .) It's true that I wore my stories of heartache, booze and ignominy on my sleeve like a wound. I talked about blackouts and paying for sex and falling over and apart. I may have been in a man's world, even trying to act like one, but my material has always been very female: messy, emotional and vulnerable.

I didn't feel that I degraded myself in my show *Judith Lucy versus Men* but not everyone agreed. A gay male friend of mine said that when I told my collection of buggerlugs stories, he thought a lot of women in the audience felt sorry for me. I've no idea if that's true but sympathy certainly wasn't my intention. The show was meant to highlight the behaviour that I've been complicit in when chasing a man, while also making the point that I was now done with it. But the message was clearly lost on a lot of people, as every night the audience overwhelmingly voted for me to keep dating.

Even when I did publicity, all the interviewers, off air, said pretty much the same thing to me: 'You don't mean it, you wouldn't really stop wanting to meet someone?' Although there was the older male interviewer who said to me, on air, that maybe the reason I didn't have a man was because I'd always been a 'bit of a good-time girl'. What a lovely, quaint, old-fashioned way of calling me a slut.

A couple of very thoughtful men, on hearing an interview with me, offered to help out; a 73-year-old from Brisbane said he'd have sex with me, and a man from South Australia also said he'd have a go, even though he'd been celibate for fifteen years. It would be good to know if the lack of sex was his idea or the rest of the world's.

Some people might think I shouldn't be so hasty in giving up dating – anything's better than being alone, isn't it? Maybe some ladies did pity me when they saw the show, but possibly that was a defence against thinking about what they'd put up with, the compromises they'd made. Of course, we all make them in relationships, but I wonder how many women deny this until they're older, when, like my mother, it's too late to change.

A recent UN report showed that ninety per cent of the world's population are biased against women – that's a lot of women doubting themselves. The realisation that I've been guilty of that myself, by being so critical of my female peers and my own work, is also quite recent. Did I doubt that we deserved to be there? I'm rarely offered corporate gigs because they're largely for a straight male audience, so unsurprisingly I'm not their first choice. We all sell our souls a little at these gigs because we only do them for the money, but if I'm performing to a room full of accountants, say, I always start with this joke: 'I don't want to show off but I got a great review recently. It described me as looking like Michelle Pfeiffer's younger sister' – yes happy with that part of the sentence, but the rest of it was, 'if a tree had fallen on top of her.' I really did have that written about me but I'd tell it because it was my way of saying, 'Relax guys, I may be the one holding the microphone and I know it's odd that you're all having to pay attention to a woman but I'm a bit ugly and weird, so you don't have to feel threatened by me.'

I know what I'm doing – putting these men at ease at the expense of a little piece of my self-respect. All these years, I've been trying to straddle two worlds: I'm this funny feminist with internalised misogyny who doesn't really want to upset the guys, who still wants them to like her and occasionally fuck her. It's a strange thing to recognise in your fifties. I love women, and my sex has defined me as a comic, yet I think I've also desperately tried to deny it by trying to drink and fuck like a man and by finding anything other than their approval not quite enough.

Which brings me to what my real problem with *Nanette* was. I wasn't confronted because of who I am onstage but off it. I agree with Hannah that anger isn't constructive, connection is. But I needed to get angry first and I never have. I couldn't do what she did with that show – I wouldn't be comfortable performing without the affirmation of laughter a number of times a minute, the confirmation that I was doing okay – but I've also never been able to own my story the way she did. I've never been able to get that furious because I haven't been brave enough.

And, to be completely honest, I was also insanely jealous of the phenomenon that *Nanette* became. I'd played the game, I'd been funny – why hadn't I ever got that recognition? That envy stopped me from really hearing the trauma that Hannah had gone through, as did my denial about my need to please men. Watching someone who so clearly didn't give a fuck about them or their opinions put me into an absolute spin. I watched the show again recently and thought it was brilliant – and funny. I think Hannah might even be a bit of a genius.

I'm really only just waking up to a lot of this. Finally, though, in *Judith Lucy versus Men*, I held a poll that revealed, through a diminishing show of hands, that there were very few straight men in my audience. I'd finally stopped chasing the approval that I was never going to get anyway and it felt tremendous.

But I'm getting ahead of myself. It took one last disaster to make me start seeing my life in an entirely different way.

PART TWO

Having the Rug Pulled Out from Under Me

6

The Fairytale

And then I met him. My prince. And it happened just like all the magazine articles said: I wasn't actively looking for anyone, I was feeling really good about myself, and then all of a sudden I had the fairytale.

I'd never *really* believed in the fairytale and yet I still wanted it. Why? We're drip-fed it from the moment we come out of a vagina, so even when we're loaded up with feminist theory it's pretty impossible not to buy into. I remember being shocked when I heard a podcast in which a couple of young feminists discussed the marriage of Prince Harry and Meghan Markle: they were so elated. It was partly because Meghan's biracial and an activist but mainly because she was in love with and marrying her prince!

The two women even suggested that Meghan would probably have to give up publicly supporting a lot of her beliefs, including feminism, but this really didn't seem to bother them. I don't care if the royal family live or die but the hysteria over this particular union made me want to scream, 'Don't you get it? She's giving up all her independence to marry a Fanta pants whose family are shape-shifting lizards!' *The Crown* has a lot to answer for. (I didn't make it past the first couple of episodes. I thought that while the historical events were interesting, Liz and Phil weren't. It was like watching a long, beautifully produced, British version of *Forrest Gump*.)

We've obviously seen that the royal glass slipper didn't fit as well as everyone thought it would, and though this particular fairytale wasn't helped by racist tabloid newspapers, the story in fact never lives up to our fantasy. We all know that it's after the prince and princess ride off into the sunset and the credits roll that the challenges start.

Like many of my generation, I thought marriage was an archaic, misogynist institution. I get that most people who marry now don't see it as being about ownership, but it's still astonishing to me how many women change their surname. A young woman I met actually thought that you legally had to change it. Sure, she was an idiot, but unnervingly she was also a journalist.

I didn't even want children so what did I think being partnered up would give me? A guaranteed airport pickup? Before meeting my prince, I'd always been slightly disappointed when I was in a relationship. Some were with lovely men – they weren't all buggerlugs – but still,

THE FAIRYTALE

there was no sex on tap or even quite the support and companionship I'd assumed there would be. Instead there was compromise and emotional (along with financial) cost. I'm possibly sounding a bit like some men here but I did question what I was actually getting out of being with someone and I often wondered if I'd be better off single. Society told me that I could never be truly happy without a plus-one, though, and on some level I bought it. I thought it was the missing piece. When a friend of mine, who's roughly my age and has largely been on her own, suddenly and unexpectedly found herself in a relationship, her family reacted a little like she'd miraculously regained the use of her legs. Despite my own experience and countless examples of terrible unions, including the one I grew up with, deep down I still thought, like millions before me, that meeting the right person would solve all my problems.

When the long-term relationship before I met my prince had ended I was totally desperate. I was just about to turn forty and thought I may as well buy a T-shirt with *Hi, I'm a crazy cat lady just without the cats* written on it. I had to meet someone NOW, before it was too late! I went on a couple of dates with a lame duck, had a fling and a couple of other casual encounters but nothing substantial. After being rejected by a younger man who'd passed out in my bed after a night of partying (I mean, come on, I just assumed that he was a welcome gift from the hotel), I finally started to calm the fuck down. There was nothing I could do about spinsterhood, so it was time to take control of the rest of my life and try to feel good about it. I was back at school again; I was powerless with respect to boyfriends but I could work hard and get good grades. I made a TV series, *Judith Lucy's Spiritual Journey*, which proved to be the best working experience of my life. I also wrote a book based on it, toured a successful show and moved to Sydney.

I changed cities mainly to prove I wasn't stuck, now that I was middle-aged, and to see if the Emerald City, for which I've always had a very big soft spot, could be my home. The only times I'd spent significant periods there was when I relocated for radio gigs, and I wanted to stop whining about the weather in Melbourne and see if Sydney was where I belonged. If I'm honest, I also wondered, despite not having one close straight friend there at the time, whether a change of scene might result in meeting someone too. I did fall in love, very hard in fact – with Melbourne.

Sydney is an incredible place but it's not my home, and the greatest gift it gave me was that realisation. Specifically, Bondi Beach gave it to me. I was walking around there one afternoon, surrounded by gorgeous, thin, tanned people, and suddenly felt like one of the extras in the miniseries *Chernobyl*. It was time to get back to the city where being pasty and covering up your body is hip.

I'd lasted eighteen months in New South Wales and by the time I returned I was feeling pretty good about life. I moved back into my old suburb and I remember very clearly walking home from a yoga class on a summer night and thinking, I'm happy. While deep down, I don't think

THE FAIRYTALE

I'd given up on the fairytale, I wasn't out there pursuing it. I was forty-four, my second book was about to come out, and my friend Denise Scott and I were about to start work on our first show as a duo. Life was good.

Not long afterwards I paid a visit to my old video store. It was one of the best in Melbourne and I still miss it. It had terrific arthouse and nostalgia sections, but maybe the greatest thing about it was the staff. Most of them were movie nerds of course and all of them were men. I'm not sure I ever got to the bottom of that – I believe there'd been a woman employed there once and it had ended badly. Maybe a nerd caught sight of one of her tampons, or she'd confessed to liking *Beaches*.

They were all very interesting gentlemen, though, and that place spawned an actor, musicians and an academic. Those guys were also a little intimidating, and for a long time I never spoke to any of them except when making a transaction. (This was also because I often went in there when I was hungover and not wearing a bra.) I knew that every film choice was noted. One particularly nauseous day I got out a selection of pretty terrible chick flicks that I just wanted to eat in front of and cry to. When I went up to the counter, I said to the man, 'Please don't judge me.' And he replied, 'Oh . . . I'm judging you.'

He was my favourite. Let's call him Mr Rabbit, because I can't keep calling him my prince. Yes, it was he. (Also, we wound up doing a podcast together called 'Mr Rabbit and the Bearded Lady' – news on my face shaving to come!)

We might never have had a proper conversation but for the fact that I was once in the shop during the day and heard him say that his number-one Australian film is *Wake in Fright*. It's also mine, which I mentioned when I took up my rentals. I should have paid more attention to the title that brought us together, but we spoke often after that and I always enjoyed the chats and his recommendations. When he told me he wasn't studying or pursuing something else as well I was surprised, because he was clearly very smart and knew an awful lot about movies. I wonder where the Quentin Tarantinos of tomorrow work now?

I never thought of him much when I wasn't in the store, though. I certainly never considered him a romantic option as he's twelve years younger than me, although I was saddened the day he told me he was leaving to go overseas for the first time, now that he was turning thirty. He said he'd told only his favourite customers he was going – I got a little buzz from that, and a bigger one when he said he was going to finish the day early because he wanted to end on serving someone he liked. We said vague things about Facebook and I never expected to see him again. He went to Europe and I moved to Sydney not long after.

Imagine my surprise when I walked back into the building a couple of years later and there he was behind the counter. I'd had the impression that his trip was meant to be the circuit-breaker that ended his career in video stores, so I said, 'What are you doing here?' It turned out that his trip had lasted just six weeks (I later realised it was

THE FAIRYTALE

an example of 'no matter where you go, there you are') and he'd only swung by the shop to pick up some boxes; he was moving into a studio apartment. We talked for a while and I recall thinking I should suggest we go out for a drink, but couldn't quite manage it. The end of the conversation was excruciating. I later discovered he'd been thinking about asking me for a drink too. I walked away feeling a little disappointed with myself, and vowing that if I ever bumped into him again I would ask him out, as a friend. And a few days later, walking down the same street as the video store, I did. We exchanged numbers.

Mr Rabbit is not a very sociable person, and for him to make that first drinks meeting happen was a big deal. He'd written the date down on a wall calendar. We met at a local bar and things were nice but unremarkable, then I had to leave to see the Paul Thomas Anderson film *The Master* with a friend. As I sat there hating it, I wondered how Mr Rabbit could have sat through it several times. (I remember thinking that maybe our relationship needed the counter between us, it couldn't survive in the wild. It was a bit like seeing a chemist at eye level, without the white coat or my script for hormone replacement therapy, but more on that later.)

He contacted me again in that strange week between Christmas and New Year, and having nothing on I agreed to meet him. Neither of us were drinking at that point and I may even have been considering calling it a day when the subject of family came up. I said, 'Well, if we're going to talk about our families I'm going to need a glass of wine.' Many hours and stories of dysfunction later, he was back at my place and we were kissing.

We had a couple of false starts, where we took it in turns to freak out about being together, but one night he turned up with a gift of fancy butter, as opposed to chocolates, and I remember thinking that I should stop worrying and just enjoy whatever this was. Here was a man who understood my love of fat and salt.

And that was how I started going out with the guy from my local video store. It was like something from an eighties rom-com. He was John Cusack to my Ione Skye, although given the age difference maybe I would've been played by Cher. That twelve-year gap was an issue for me – for months I assumed we were having a fling. It wasn't that he lacked maturity or that shared references were a problem; he had siblings my age and generally seemed an old soul. It was more that I had an established career and had (hopefully) worked some shit out, which he was yet to do. At one point Kevin, my manager, assured me that because of his hair loss, Mr Rabbit looked at least four years older, which was a real comfort.

My concern that he was yet to work stuff out proved quite an understatement. At the ten-month mark, just when I was starting to relax, he broke up with me. He appeared at my door pretty demented, not having slept for at least two nights, saying he would have to end it, he was just 'incapable' of being with me. I knew this was entirely due to his depression,

THE FAIRYTALE

but although it wasn't the first time he'd shut down or pulled back, it was still a shock. I was devastated – just as I was getting over my issues, we ran smack-bang into his.

Over the next three months we slowly patched things back together. Possibly we just never should have, but although he'd bruised me badly the truth is, he'd treated me better than any man ever had. I cared for him deeply. He was supportive, physically demonstrative, and appeared to be completely at ease with the inequity of our careers and finances. 'It's because he's younger,' my friends would say. 'The generation below us are so much more relaxed with their masculinity.'

His blind spot was the sexism in some of the movies he showed me, maybe because he'd never been taught to view them from a feminist angle, and to his credit, once he became aware he was appalled. I remember him telling me, while we were slowly negotiating our reconciliation, that he owed me a grand gesture. I kept waiting for him to appear with a boom box outside my window playing a Peter Gabriel track if hiring a skywriter was too expensive, but the truth was I was desperate to have him back.

On our second go-round we grew closer than ever. I've never had so much in common with a partner or spent so much time with one person. Where had this guy come from? Could I clone him for my single friends? Far from being threatened by his funny lady's achievements, he celebrated them. I would even read him material I'd written and ask his opinion about jokes. I hadn't subjected ANYONE to this before. We did a podcast about movies together and we were writing a play. We'd become those people who are always referred to as a couple. My friends loved him. What was left of my family loved him and he really couldn't have been more spectacular when my brother was dying. His empathy and support, not just for me but for everyone close to Niall, seemed another testament to his maturity. That experience meant that I not only trusted him more than anyone I'd ever dated, but came to rely on him in a way that was completely new.

I knew it was ridiculous to think that you could have all your needs met by one person, unless it was a robot that combined Aaron Pedersen, Stephen Colbert and a porn star, but Mr Rabbit blew all that out of the water. I remember saying to friends, 'I finally understand what people are talking about when they say that a healthy relationship can make your life better.' I had met my soulmate. I never expected it to be the guy from the video store but who cared? He shared my interests but unlike so many other men I'd been drawn to, he wasn't competing with me.

I was a version of myself that I'd never been with anyone else. I didn't feel like I was on trial anymore. One of the films he'd judged me for renting was *Waiting to Exhale* but that's how I felt, like I could truly relax with this person. Gradually, and really for the first time in my life, I started to think that he was my 'forever'. I'm embarrassed to admit that I even gave him a card saying just that, with a drawing

THE FAIRYTALE

of an elderly couple holding hands, staring out to sea. (Obviously when I was in my twenties I gave guys cards that said, 'You're my next six hours,' with a sketch of me throwing up on myself in a cab on the way home.)

Made it Ma, top of the world! It wasn't Gavin or Gareth, Mum! But I found him! The One, Mr Right, my Prince Charming! He'd taken his time but he was here.

The year after my brother died I wrote and performed a stand-up show called *Ask No Questions of the Moth*. Touring was still a grind but the panic attacks were much better, the show was a success, and I more or less enjoyed performing it. Most importantly, it was a lot less lonely because Mr Rabbit would either come with me or be at the end of the phone after a show. And when I was performing in Melbourne, I can't tell you what it was like to know that I wouldn't be going home to an empty flat, and that there'd be a meal prepared and a bottle of wine open. There he was again, making my life better. I was madly in love.

He still hadn't given up his studio apartment, even though he was rarely there, but finally we agreed that he would move in with me and we'd start saving to buy somewhere together. I didn't care that I'd be paying the lion's share and used to joke that he would have to support me when I was old and infirm.

I'd only ever lived with men in the past because of 'circumstances' (such as when one of the walls of my rental was replaced with clear plastic as part of a renovation; I'm not saying I wasn't in love with the boyfriend I was forced to move in with, but it was terrific that you couldn't see into his shower from the street) and I'd never made long-term plans about the future with anyone.

It wasn't perfect. We needed help in the bedroom but I mainly put this down to falling out of the habit when my brother was sick. There was a lot of affection, though, and I felt sure we'd figure this out. For a year he was unemployed, which was difficult, but then he got two jobs, and while not career-making, they paid the bills. He had an outlet for his talents in the play we were writing and the podcast we were doing, which was gaining an audience. We'd even done a live show at the Woodford Folk Festival, where he did a remarkably good job for someone with no experience of performing.

There was another problem, though. One of the other things we had in common was our pretty screwed-up families, hence the ten hours of drinking on one of our early dates. Despite his age and his interests and the thoughtful words of my friends, masculinity *was* a very big issue for him, because of his upbringing. He had a strange notion about being a 'perfect boyfriend'. I wasn't sure what that was meant to entail, other than torturing himself over an impossible ideal (I'm assuming that not living up to this was why he broke it off with me the first time). It's a paradoxical ideal at that, because it sounds like it's all about the other person when it's actually about what you think the female and male roles should be. I thought he'd stopped thinking like that but it turned out he hadn't.

THE FAIRYTALE

It's not like I had my own shit perfectly together either. I was still grieving Niall, I'd become estranged from my sister-in-law and her two children, and sometimes I was all too aware of being twelve years older than my partner. I was once mistaken for his mother; thankfully I had the presence of mind to turn to the young shop assistant and say, 'I love that kid, but between you and me he's a lousy fuck.' Actually I didn't say that but it made a good routine. Menopause had kicked in, too, emphasising the age difference, and my job wasn't making me feel great either.

Working on a new show with Denise Scott was as enjoyable as ever but one of the reasons it was called *Disappointments* was because we'd both recently experienced a few. One of mine was having a TV show rejected, and I was very much feeling like my career had gone right off the boil. On top of all this it was getting more and more difficult to ignore the fact that the world was going to hell in a handbasket. I did ignore it, though.

In truth, my relationship was the only part of my life I felt really good about, but it made up for everything. I HAD A MAN. I was part of a couple, we were busy hanging out with other couples and going to farmers' markets. Everything else would sort itself out in good time.

Towards the fifth anniversary of my relationship with Mr Rabbit, Scotty and I were in Brisbane on the final leg of our tour for that year. We used to joke that our show about failure and regrets kept writing itself, and it was about to hand me another terrible chapter. My very silly job means

I often get paid in lump sums, which I split into one bank account that I live on and another reserved for the taxation department. I rarely look at that second one because it's money I can't spend. On the Friday of our last weekend of shows for 2017, my management contacted me to say there wasn't enough money in the account to pay my tax. I said that couldn't possibly be true and the accountant replied, 'Yes, well, you have been making all those withdrawals.' No, I hadn't.

I got off the phone and rang my bank, which was able to tell me very quickly that tens of thousands had been going into Mr Rabbit's account. I was convinced this was some error on the bank's part; in fact, I spent twenty-four hours in complete denial, which at least made performing the show achievable. Mr Rabbit also made that easier by refuting all knowledge, although at one point he conceded that some money had gone into his account but he'd assumed it was a gift from me. I still didn't believe the obvious fact that was virtually grabbing me by the shoulders and shaking me.

Later that night I said to Scotty, 'Tell me honestly, what do you think has happened?' She said quietly, 'I think he's fucked you over.' (A couple of years later she told me that when she said that, I looked like I wanted to slap her across the face.)

The next day, I rang Mr Rabbit and said, 'I just want to make sure you're okay because I realise this all sounds like I'm accusing you of something, and I know you'd never do anything like that.' He replied, 'I can't keep gaslighting

THE FAIRYTALE

you. I've been stealing money out of your account for over two years.'

I will never forget that sentence as long as I live.

My memory of what happened after that is very foggy. I think I rang a couple of friends, maybe Jan, and then I met up with Scotty and told her she'd been right. Mainly I remember having to perform two shows on the Saturday and one on the Sunday. I had to listen to Scotty say the insults in our mock argument, which was the turning point of the show; lines like 'Your boyfriend only goes out with you because you pay for everything.' I wrote that. It was funny at the time.

I went from thinking I was about to move in with the man I loved to thinking, I'm single again, I have a lot less money, I'm now uncertain about almost everything and I'm about to turn fifty. Shit. Not that I could have put together a sentence that coherent at the time. I don't believe I've ever been so completely blindsided, and considering the whole adoption story, that's really saying something.

I was in a state of shock for months, and there's still a part of me, writing this over three years later, that just can't fathom it. Even with the buggerlugs who'd supposedly left his wife but hadn't, I'd been able to look back over the relationship and admit that I hadn't entirely trusted him. But there was nothing like that with Mr Rabbit. I'd always thought of him as one of the most moral people I'd ever met. (He hadn't even let me off late fines at the video store, for crying out loud.) Even allowing for his depression, it was still difficult to understand what he'd done.

Early on in our relationship he'd actually told me about people who'd borrowed money from him and not returned it, and some who'd stolen his money outright, and how incomprehensible he'd found it. (Thank god he hadn't said, 'And of course I would *never* murder my girlfriend.') I, in turn, had talked about my history with men (*see* Buggerlugs) and finances (*see also* Buggerlugs), confident that I'd finally met someone who would never exploit me in that way. In case you're wondering, he knew my internet-banking password because when I had to change it I'd DISCUSSED IT WITH HIM, without giving it a second thought. I was going to grow old with this guy, why wouldn't I tell him my password?

I returned from Brisbane after the bombshell to be greeted not by him at the door, wrapping his arms around me, but by some emptied shelves and his set of keys on the kitchen bench. He came around later and it's difficult to say who looked worse. It was clear neither of us had been sleeping. I know that I felt removed from what was happening – I couldn't quite compute that the last time I'd seen this man he was a huge part of my future but now everything we had was in the past.

We had a longer version of the conversation we'd already had on the phone. There didn't really seem to be a reason for his betrayal. He'd thought I wouldn't want him if he had to borrow more money or couldn't pay for meals or

THE FAIRYTALE

bottles of wine. If he wasn't a 'perfect boyfriend'. It didn't make sense that he'd risk everything we had to fulfil his idea of what it meant to be a man. It still doesn't, but applying logic to a mind dealing with depression and other issues is never going to work. In my heart, I couldn't see a way of going back to where we were but we went to see my counsellor anyway, because I thought it might make the process of uncoupling somehow easier. I'll never forget something Mr Rabbit said during one of those sessions: 'I find out what people want then I give it to them, and then hopefully they'll leave me alone.'

Was this what a perfect partner did? Met their loved one's needs to the point of disappearing? I didn't think that described our relationship at all, but it did make me doubt everything about it. How much of him had been playing a role for me? Where did that start and end? The therapy only served to underscore my dislocation and the complete hopelessness of the situation. Whatever this man needed, I couldn't give it to him.

For the first few months after the split, I kept a diary of sorts – boy, does that make for some embarrassing reading. It's also very repetitive; every few pages I wrote that I was 'feeling like something in me had shifted'. It sounds like one of my lungs had moved into a better apartment.

I constantly seesawed between believing I'd turned a corner and plunging back into despair. I couldn't stop trying to make sense of what he'd done, even though I knew that was pointless, and there was simply no way to square his actions with his love for me. It would have been so much simpler if he'd just been a cunt – I would have moved on so much more quickly if he'd been some sort of sociopath who preyed on older ladies with the intention of draining their bank accounts. But it seemed that underneath his deception and theft was not avarice or malice, but affection. I knew that we still loved each other and yet he had made it impossible for us to be together. It was a real motherfucker.

I stopped going to the movies for a long time, because that was something we'd done together, discussing everything like David and Margaret on *At the Movies*. I struggled to even watch television for the same reason. There are certain films I'll never watch again because they remind me of him, just as there are songs that will always be too difficult to listen to because they remind me of Niall. As I write this, I still miss Mr Rabbit terribly and mourn what we had. I always will. We've met up a few times to see if we can be friends, but it doesn't seem likely.

I said that there were no clues, but actually there were. It's a little like when you're really engrossed in a movie, you'll forgive the odd lapse of credibility or the boom-mic-in-shot scene because you care about what happens – those things are just details. But I was ignoring a lot of microphones and some pretty glaring continuity mistakes.

How did I honestly think he was getting by the year he didn't have a job, even if I was footing a lot of the bills? I'd learnt my lesson about joint bank accounts, so how did I think he was paying for meals when we went out? When he sometimes shouted our friends as well, I could hear a very faint alarm bell ringing. But I convinced myself he was just maxing out his credit card or had some money saved somehow.

People would comment on his generosity. Let him pay, I'd thought, it's obviously making him feel good. When I look back at all this it makes me feel stupid, but doesn't every relationship involve some degree of fooling ourselves? It seems like every woman I know has admitted, after a break-up, the disconcerting signs that were there from the start. You don't tell your friends at the time because you know they'd say, 'You found a severed hand in his laundry basket? Honey, that is not good.'

I had to admit to myself that, along with the play, I did the movie podcast only because of him. I enjoyed talking about films but not as much as I loved seeing him grow into a critic and presenter. Women excel at thinking we can be not just a lover but everything from a career counsellor to a nutritionist for our partner. Often while we're failing at 'fixing' them, we're pretty good at breaking ourselves.

I know it would not be easy to be inside Mr Rabbit's head but sometimes it's hard to figure out where his mental-health concerns end and selfishness begins. Sometimes I think I'm still just playing the part of guest star in his tragedy. At first my sadness was entirely about missing him, then it was about the possibility that I'd never be with anyone again, and finally it was about realising how much time I'd wasted on pursuing that whole idea.

Along with the grief there was also my old friend, repressed anger. I don't recall ever raising my voice since all this happened. I feel like I have so much rage but I don't know where to put it. I just sit with it and sit with it and do my fucking meditation and cry and read up about those wrecking rooms where you can pay fifty bucks to just go and smash stuff up for half an hour.

When the relationship ended, I didn't think, Right, I need to get my act together. Sure, I've done a lot of work on myself but I'm not Dr Phil. Instead I thought something more or less along the lines of, I need to get out of this flat and off my face for a few weeks.

First I went to Sydney, stayed with friends and was drunk for a week or so. I even took some MDMA. My buddy had taken the day off work and we went out for a lovely lunch. We came home, watched television, ate pizza with his partner, and just at the point when I was considering calling it a night, my friend suggested taking the drugs, two apiece. What we did then was completely incredible: we danced to eighties break-up songs on YouTube. Isn't that reassuring? You don't stop taking drugs as you get older, you just don't leave the house anymore. I guess the next step is taking drugs and not leaving your bed. I think that's called palliative care.

I followed this trip with one to Perth, where aside from catching up with a couple of friends, I lay on Jan's couch

THE FAIRYTALE

and ate her wonderful food. Then I went to Byron Bay where I stayed with my astrologer friend, Sue, and offset my drinking with some marijuana oil. I may have been panicking about money but I had racked up some frequent flyer points and boy, did I make the most of it. Take that, Elizabeth Gilbert; who needs twelve months in Italy, India and Indonesia? I only needed a month in Sydney, Perth and Byron. After that I was fine!

I was still a mess.

After those first few weeks, I did try to look after myself. Yoga was a way to breathe and move a little and not think. Which isn't to say I was trying to avoid my feelings, I just wanted to feel them without the endless mental loops – yoga helped with that a great deal. It was the only activity that held my attention. That and masturbating. I hadn't been remotely interested in sex for months, but now that there was no one to have it with I couldn't get enough of my right hand.

Predictably I bought a self-help book, called *We: A Manifesto for Women Everywhere*. In my defence, I thought I'd probably get some jokes out of it – and I did, just not enough. It's written by Gillian Anderson, yes, *that* Gillian Anderson, Scully from *The X-Files*. Let me tell you, the truth might be out there but it's not in this fucking book. Zing!

My buddies were amazing, as usual, apart from when one of them took me shopping to cheer me up. I tried on the dress she insisted would make me look amazing and her reaction was, 'You have got to buy that . . . because you might lose some weight.' Disaster used to be slimming, but somewhere in my forties I'd discovered comfort eating. I knew I never should have given up smoking. This was the only time since stopping that I truly missed it. Eight consecutive chest infections followed by watching my brother die of lung cancer had really halted my cravings, but all of a sudden I longed for that wonderful physical act of emotional suppression. Mercifully I opted for a different kind of deep breathing instead, and once I upped the yoga difficulty I did slim down. I only mention this because when I was still feeling terrible, everyone said, 'You look great!' Jesus, fingers crossed for a tumour, gotta stay trim!

Breaking down in tears during a Pilates session a couple of months after the split summed up my life at that point. How much more middle-aged, middle-class and sad (albeit with incredible core strength) could I get? Thankfully, the class was all women and I was grateful to be surrounded by them.

Those early months were a balancing act between sitting home alone processing and forcing myself to go out and interact with other people, which was sometimes distracting and at other times a way of being forced to talk about it all. Occasionally that was healing but mostly I felt like I was just telling the story of the break-up over and over, without believing it. I did therapy too, naturally, and I cried every single day for at least a year.

THE FAIRYTALE

One thing that surprises me, looking back, is that I felt like talking to Niall about it. I'm not even sure why – I'd rarely turned to him for emotional support in our later years, but maybe it was because he'd known and liked Mr Rabbit and I thought he'd have shared my incredulity. Or maybe I thought that one enigmatic man could shed light on another and he might've been able to explain it all to me. When, a couple of days before Niall died, Mr Rabbit arrived and my sister-in-law told my unconscious brother that he was in the room, Niall stirred, shook his hand, waved at his son and stepson at the foot of the bed and even patted the dog, Johnny, on the head. He acknowledged every male in the room and managed to ignore his wife, stepdaughter and me, the three people who'd been doing the most for him.

Mr Rabbit kept a part of himself at arm's length. Like my brother, he loved secrets and I think for similar reasons – secrets are a form of withholding that gives you the upper hand, a way of inoculating yourself from the feelings of powerlessness experienced as a child – and for that reason it never really bothered me. Mr Rabbit once told me he had one secret that he would never tell anyone, which possibly should have concerned me more than it did at the time. It turns out he had an entire inner life that I knew nothing of. I've often thought about how much energy it must've taken to present himself as completely on top of everything when he was actually flailing. Women are programmed to do the opposite, to show our love by opening ourselves up and giving ourselves away.

Despite how complex humans are, we crave simple explanations. I've tried to capture a larger part of who Mr Rabbit is because it would be wrong if all I wrote about was his deception. People have told me they think I've been 'amazing' about it all, or too forgiving, but the truth is, who he is forces that response. I can't just dismiss him as an awful person because he isn't. He has a flaw that neither of us could escape. For my own part, I held him up as the key that had unlocked the door to my happiness. He didn't want me to see that he was struggling but I didn't want to see it either. I just wanted him to fit in with my career, my friends and my life, and he did. I needed him to be the anti-buggerlugs, to take all the inequities in our relationship in his stride.

He would talk about me having high standards and I would laugh it off, because at the time I couldn't see that it wasn't just me who I was holding to those standards. Maybe, after years of disappointment, I *had* wanted him to be perfect.

The relationship was a great cover for both of us. Neither of us had to deal with our own demons while we were together. I've never been the sort of person to put my friends or career on the backburner when a man was around, but Christ, it took up mental space; I spent so much time thinking about him and us, from what we were going to do that night to when did he last call his mother to what would we do for Christmas.

When I finally came out the other side of the initial shock and sadness, I realised how he'd enabled me to hide

THE FAIRYTALE

from the parts of my life I wasn't too happy about, because finally a man had 'completed me'. But there they were, all my doubts and disillusions, sitting on top of other stuff I hadn't even known I'd been avoiding, all underlined by the fact that I was fifty and alone.

The rug had been completely pulled from underneath me, and for the next couple of years it felt like each time I steadied myself it would be pulled out again. There was absolutely nothing to hold onto. Every single part of my life was up for grabs. My anguish was replaced by panic and to make matters worse, the universe seemed to keep reminding me that time was running out. For what? When I say the universe, I really mean my vagina. Menopause had knocked me for six, in a way I hadn't anticipated, and I could no longer hide from that either. I felt old, undesirable and dry. The fairytale had been just a fucking fairytale.

7
Short-changed
Falling Apart Physically

Ignoring my changing body was no mean feat, considering I take it with me just about everywhere. I hadn't been able to completely ignore the physical changes I was going through while I was with Mr R but it makes a big difference when the reflection you see in the mirror is tempered by the one you see in a loving partner's eyes. Someone still finding you attractive is an enormous salve against aging. When I didn't have that anymore a natural process suddenly seemed like a decline, one that mocked the idea that I could ever be seen as desirable again. I felt like I was falling apart and so was my body.

When Mr Rabbit and I were together, we'd had a counselling session about our sex life where I admitted how much menopause was affecting my confidence in that area. I'd always been one of those women fortunate enough to get wet pretty easily (note to self: don't ever write porn), but suddenly that wasn't happening. If I'm honest, I was also a little bereaved about not being able to have children with Mr R, which surprised me. I'd never wanted them and here I was, forty-six, but weirdly I still wanted the option. No, I didn't – I just didn't want to feel old.

Thanks to our bodies, women have a much more loaded relationship with time than guys do. I didn't want to think about how my skin was going to lose its elasticity and my bones were going to get less dense and my libido was going to disappear. It was a relief to talk openly about it; Mr R had no idea that was how I'd been feeling. So even though it was only my genitals that felt so dry Clint Eastwood could have struck a match on them to light his cheroot, it felt like my partner and I were going to deal with this *together*.

I've read that one of the reasons women deal better with their mortality is because the onset of menopause is a very big wake-up call. Now that I was without a partner, it sounded more like a death wail marking the end of all possibility.

It seems to me no accident that the natural decline in reproductive hormones is called MENopause, because for those poor suckers among us who are attracted to guys, feeling that we're no longer desirable to the opposite sex is a big part of it. Although 'pause' sounds like you're having an intermission when it comes to blokes, whereas the reality can feel more like the feature film is over and the cinema just burnt down.

Everyone's journey with their withering ovaries is different, but one thing we all share is that none of us want to kick off our dating profile with, 'I have a terrific sense of humour and a dry vagina.' And I think we've established that a lot of men don't really care about the sense of humour. It's another of life's crazy ironies that just when you can finally stop worrying about getting pregnant you no longer desire sex, and/or men don't desire you because you're now a 'woman of a certain age'.

I can't actually quite believe that I'm fifty-two. I did a corporate gig recently and as a way of getting to a joke, I mentioned that I was over fifty and the whole room APPLAUDED. Were they as surprised as me that I'm still alive? A friend told me I should be thrilled that fifty doesn't mean what it used to. When her father hit that milestone, his supposed friends threw him a party and gave him a walking stick. Why didn't they just put a gun to his head and shoot him?

When you're younger fifty might as well be three hundred and twelve. Part of the reason I can't believe I'm in my sixth decade is because three close friends died at forty-seven, so just making it to forty-eight was thrilling. I wasn't elated at hitting half a century, though. Turning forty didn't bother me much but there's no getting around the fact that when you hit the big five-zero, there's less time ahead of you than there is behind, and while it seems to be around this age that some men embark on their second families with a younger partner, few women are being complimented for their 'distinguished looks' and impressive careers. My friend Robyn nailed it when she said, 'Let's face it, Jude, some of us are just past our use-by date.' Odd, isn't it? Men aren't referred to as cartons of milk that have gone off.

Most of the articles I read on women my age revolve around how I should be feeling about my marriage and my children moving out of home. As that's not my experience, have I somehow failed? Recently a seventy-year-old Ukrainian taxi driver asked me if I had kids, and when I said I didn't he immediately felt the need to say, 'Every life is made up of the bitter and the sweet. I'm sure that you have other things.' Like what? Cutlery?

One of the many clichés that's true about getting older is that you still think you're thirty-five, or whatever age you like, and have many years ahead of you, so when a young gentleman offered me a seat on the train recently it was as if he knew a secret that I thought only a handful of people were in on, and it wasn't that I was pregnant. How did he know my age? Who'd told him? Surely it wasn't obvious from how I *looked*? Naturally I declined his offer, and had to fight the instinct to say, 'I do yoga, I'm really vital, I still go and see bands and take drugs, so thanks but no thanks and how about a date?'

Then my doctor told me I have arthritis in my knees and possibly my hands. I can't say any more about this because I've decided it simply didn't happen.

When my brother died, I became menopausal pretty much overnight. I was forty-six. The average age in Australia for this is fifty-one, so it took me a while to work out what was happening. Wasn't there meant to be something before that? Wasn't I meant to first get weird, unruly periods and erratic symptoms and then be menopausal? Wasn't there some PERi-PERi chicken from Nando's or something? I simply wasn't prepared!

As it turned out, I didn't have a period for two and a half years – I mean, not a drop – and *then* I started to get the weird half-periods, even some very heavy ones again. I was just all out of whack. You really haven't lived until you've dealt with being menopausal and having a period; if only I'd been up the duff as well, I could have had the trifecta. I've always had a tendency towards insomnia and anxiety, and when those things got worse while Niall was sick, I didn't really know if they were caused by my hormones going nuts or not.

How can my own body still be such a mystery to me? I know I'm not the only woman who, even after thirty years, was still vaguely surprised whenever I got a period. Oh, I'd think, that's why I was a bit sad.

When it finally dawned on me that it was the 'change of life' (why is no other part of your life, like adolescence, referred to as a change? Why don't they just call menopause 'short-changed', 'wrong change' or 'vulva declined'?) and I'd had it confirmed by a doctor, I was horrified at all the other potential symptoms: difference in body odour, hair loss, incontinence and ATROPHY OF THE VAGINA, to name a few of my favourites. Some women's hot flushes are so extreme, according to one article I read, they actually feel they're being engulfed by flames. Stop screaming, Joan of Arc, it's just hormonal!

Symptoms like urge incontinence (when the bladder develops a mind of its own – who needs a toilet, there's a shoe!) can make you feel a whole lot less fetching, no matter how many magazines tell you that fifty is the new forty and forty the new thirty. One helpful article I read about staying vibrant said, 'Eat more fruit. Fruit is sexy, period.' Oh my god, that's the answer! Pass me a pineapple! Just get fucked. I realised that we 'mature' women must all be reading the same pieces on how to look twenty-seven again when I noticed a number of us with glamorous painted nails. Apparently this makes your hands look younger. I was hoping that they distracted from my face. For the same reason, I've also taken to wearing clogs, a loincloth and a poncho. I'm actually surprised I haven't seen a middle-aged woman sporting that look along with pink hair, crazy glasses frames and a sign that says, 'FOR THE LOVE OF GOD, LOOK AT ME! I AM NOT INVISIBLE.'

I understand this desperation. I completely panicked after the break-up. For starters, I thought very seriously about dying my hair blonde. In fact, it struck me as ridiculous that I hadn't done it before. I mean, that was obviously the problem – all I needed was a packet of Clairol Nice 'N Easy Ash Blonde and I could really turn the whole feeling-unattractive ship around. I came to my senses on that one; I actually like my dark hair with its grey streaks, and as is often the case with me and grooming, I just couldn't be arsed.

With each passing year, I become more sympathetic to the idea of cosmetic procedures. I've always railed against them in my work, I hate the fact that women having toxins injected into themselves, or surgery for the sake of a flat stomach or taut jawline has been so normalised. How has the natural process of aging been turned into something we're meant to fight? I know, because there's a lot of money to be made, but WE'RE ALL GOING TO DIE. Get as many facelifts as you want, they're not going to stop your body changing and eventually giving up on you, because that's what it's meant to do. Fillers, botox, they all work for a while but then you fall off a cliff. I thought Sandra Bullock looked great for years and then I saw her at some awards ceremony recently and thought, My god she looks like a wooden puppet of Pinocchio. So do a lot of celebrities.

What is it about all that work that just makes you look identical to all the other aging stars who've had it done too? I really can't tell Madeleine Stowe from Terri Hatcher anymore. And I can't read another article about celebrities who are 'Over Fifty and Fabulous', with photos of people like Madonna, our Nic and Sharon Stone. They don't look fabulous. As the wonderful Kaz Cooke says, 'These days when you age you have a choice, you can look old or you can look weird.'

It drives me yet more bananas when cosmetic procedures aren't even acknowledged. I read an article about

J.Lo's amazing performance at the Super Bowl. The author, an older woman, was lamenting the fact that now we're all going to have to look like the singer and be able to pole-dance at fifty. She mentioned Jennifer's genes and the money that enables her to have personal trainers, but not the fact that Jenny from the block has used more fillers than a wall repairer. I can't even be bothered questioning why writhing around on a slippery silver phallus is somehow meant to be empowering.

Having said all that, when I became single again I went to see a dermatologist. It was medical; I mean, I had a referral from a GP. I didn't want my muscles to be frozen or my face to be plumped but I was keen to hear if there was anything non-invasive I could do to make me look thirty years younger. I also had some incredible notion that a woman who makes money out of other women's insecurities was going to tell me I looked good for my age and shouldn't worry about it. She didn't. She herself looked like a kewpie doll. Her skin was so smooth and ghostly white that I wondered if she should be out of her coffin during the day.

I mainly saw this skin specialist because the area around my mouth was making me look more and more like Caesar from the *Planet of the Apes* movies. She told me that my years of smoking hadn't helped, obviously, but the real problem was that I'd used the muscles around my lips too much. (I knew I shouldn't have blown so many guys; even my face is punishing me.) She actually told me I'd done too much TALKING. Who knew? Living is in fact aging me. I must cut that out.

One solution the dermatologist suggested for my mouth was a series of needling treatments; this is where, yes, they stick needles into your face, which makes it bleed so that the skin is 'shocked' into producing more collagen. You can't go out in the sun for several days after you've had it done, and it's not cheap or, of course, permanent. She also armed me with some cream that I was going to have to put on my face every night for the rest of my life.

What the fuck are we doing to ourselves? Women have penis facials, wear masks made out of bird crap and get covered in their own blood to look younger. You can now do yoga for the face, which is meant to keep it pubescent-looking and nubile, and there's also a 'gym' for the visage where essentially you're pummelled and pulled, and, again, it's all meant to rejuvenate and refresh. In the end, I didn't do the needling. Hats off to you if you have, I just couldn't justify it financially and I stopped using the magic cream because even after a few months it was still stinging when I applied it and it made my skin peel. I didn't look younger, I just looked like I was decomposing.

I was surprised by how much all of this bothered me. As a feminist and a lover of the title of Judge Judy's book, *Beauty Fades, Dumb is Forever*, I honestly didn't think that wrinkles would trouble me, nor the fact that my neck is starting to look like something you'd see in the reptile enclosure at the zoo. There are so many other reminders of my physical decline too: my teeth continue to turn the colour of Jarlsberg cheese, my receding gums require constant flossing and sluicing, my bunions are flourishing, capillaries become more and more visible, and overall skin dryness has meant I probably could've finished this book a month or two earlier if I didn't have to spend so much time applying moisturiser.

Oh, and I now have to shave my face. I looked in a mirror, actually in my therapist's bathroom (is she angling for more sessions?), and was horrified to notice that in a certain light the down on my face makes me look like a bumblebee. So I BOUGHT A SHAVER. It's specifically for ladies and because of its lid looks more like an enormous lipstick, but fuck, I didn't see that one coming. No one told me I was going to look like a werewolf. I tried threading first. For some reason, a procedure in a beauty salon seemed less humiliating than succumbing to the daily ritual in front of the bathroom mirror that my father used to perform. Threading involves a woman pulling a taut piece of cotton over your face to pluck the hairs out with the dexterity of a sadistic harpist. I'd been warned it was painful, but when I bled profusely around the jawline after my second appointment, I thought there had to be a better way of not looking like a human dandelion.

The maintenance bothers me, the cost of it shits me, but I suppose more than anything it's all a constant reminder of the ticking clock (not the womb one, the one above my grave) and the reality that I couldn't possibly be attractive because I don't look twentysomething anymore. It's alarming how often it gets back to men not wanting to fuck me, but I suppose it's the thought that the few who once did certainly won't want to now, will they.

I heard an older woman once talk about the fact that she'd never thought of having neck surgery until she got sick to death of looking at ladies who she knew were older than her but who looked younger, so she succumbed because she felt so unattractive. THAT WAS JULIE CHRISTIE. I also read an interview where Kristen Scott Thomas talked about now being invisible to men. If she's invisible I must be some sort of black hole. I hate it that I still care about all of this, after all these years.

How did our mothers and their mothers before them keep silent about this stage of their lives? It brings so many humiliations, not to mention pain, depression, and let's not forget sweating, so much sweating. Why women haven't marched down the street protesting it and stabbing any man who rolled his eyes is just incredible to me. Then again, we haven't said much about menstruation and childbirth either, so why start now?

What would it be like I wonder to experience the Change away from the male gaze? How would it be if we could just accept what was happening to our bodies, instead of letting our insecurities be exploited while we continue running a race we can never win? Oh to live in a society where our hormones are not seen as an embarrassing, messy inconvenience but a beautiful part of being a woman, the giver of life. Oh to be respected and cared for when that part of your life is ending, so that you can move into the next phase of being a wiser, older attractive woman, still with desires and many things to offer. Take me back to Themyscira so I can embrace my inner crone and gleefully howl at the moon!

Women are finally starting to talk about menopause but I understand where the reticence has come from: who wants to admit to something that is tantamount to saying, 'I'm now old and useless, because according to our culture I was really only worthwhile when I was pretty and could bear children.' It's a bitch, isn't it ladies?

As I said, I've always suffered from poor sleep and stress but after years of therapy, yoga and meditation, I had them under control. Not anymore, thanks to the Change. I started to feel like I was going insane. At least in the past the anxiety usually had a reason – now it was unmoored, just a free-ranging cloud of nerves that could descend at any time. Thank Christ my naturopath said, 'Just get on HRT.' But even with that, symptoms often break through and I've had to change the prescription at least five times because a pill would suddenly stop being effective.

Another fun interlude was when my menopause-induced headaches were misdiagnosed for six months as a sinus infection, which meant spending half a year going to specialists and trying all sorts of expensive nasal sprays and antibiotics. My favourite moment was when a young female doctor put some new symptoms down to cystitis, a condition that in the past I'd associated with too much sex. Thanks to menopause I felt like I had a urinary tract infection without the preceding good times. Were women designed by someone who was trying to win a bet?

It might not be a panacea but do you know what it's like to run out of your HRT? If you weren't feeling anxious before you will be now. At one point it seemed like the entire state had run out of Femoston-Conti. I went into chemist after chemist, to have young women or men of any age look at me like I was getting hysterical because they'd run out of emery boards, as opposed to the pill that was my bridge to sanity. I did wonder if there would've been a shortage had the medication been essential to the wellbeing of middle-aged men.

All of this is complicated by the spectre of breast cancer, which I might be courting by taking HRT. Doctors had put those fears to bed to some degree, but about six months ago, new articles appeared about the link that were just terrifying. My doctor told me they were based on dated studies, but the most comforting fact she could give me was that she was still taking her HRT, so I guess we can do chemo together. Next month we'll probably read that it gives you tuberculosis and a sudden urge to compete in dressage at the World Equestrian Games.

But in the same way that ladies learn to deal with the pain, inconvenience and emotional rollercoaster of menstruating, coupled with the constant fear of pregnancy if you're sexually active, we adjust to the Change. What choice is there? Maybe the money you once spent on getting a Brazilian (no thank you) you can now spend on getting your beard waxed? Maybe the money you invested in getting a fake tan you now spend on dyeing your hair? And yes, the money you once shelled out for those luxury tampons and pads you can now spend on herbs or implants or patches or pills for menopause. I can't say I'm looking forward to death but at least it'll be cheaper and I'll stop having to think of my hormones as being a colossal pain in the arse.

Not long ago I was in a makeup room while doing a television series with a much younger woman who suffers from chronic endometriosis, and a woman who's a mother and a little older than me. Some strange alchemy happens in a makeup room, especially when there are only women there, that enables the most intimate conversations to take place. Mind you, ladies are pretty good at that under most circumstances. The three of us discussed all the iterations of pain that our hormones had subjected us to, whether it was excruciating periods, childbirth or vaginal atrophy.

We carried on like this for a good twenty minutes until there was a slight pause and the younger woman said, 'I still wouldn't be a man, though.' The other woman and I said together, 'Oh fuck no.' And we all laughed. That's something women have always had, the ability to talk and support each other with humour and empathy. When there are no men around, we can relax and not have to worry about being pretty or mysterious. We can equally revel in and be appalled by our femaleness.

I'm genuinely sorry that, as far as I can tell, a lot of straight men still don't get to experience this with each other. This shared intimacy is one of the truly great things about being a woman, yet these are snatched moments, in stark contrast to the rest of our lives. (Equal pay would be good too.) Laughing about the crazy shit our bodies put us through with other ladies is always a relief but it wasn't enough – I wanted to feel better about this lump of flesh hanging off my head and neck. I wasn't quite sure what the answer was but finding out was definitely on my to-do list. But it wasn't anywhere near the top. That honour went to, what was it again? Oh, that's right, EXISTENTIAL DREAD. Knees that looked like something from the lunar landscape were one thing, but not quite up there with wondering about THE POINT OF LIVING.

When I looked around and tried to grab onto the aspects of my life I did feel good about, I came up extremely short. I'd never experienced this total confusion before. In the past, it had felt like there was still time to work everything out, but now I felt both a sense of urgency and a kind of paralysis. Oh Jesus, don't tell me this was a complete fucking midlife crisis.

8
Is it a Duck?
More Falling Apart

While physical evidence of decline – like a wrinkle as deep as the Verdon Gorge – can be hard to ignore, the more nebulous stuff like, you know, *purpose*, is easy to push to the back of your mind when you have a play to write, a podcast to do and a host of fun social engagements!

Why worry about nagging feelings that democracy might be in a state of terminal decline, or a sense of hollowness about what you're doing with your life when there's a new Middle Eastern restaurant to try before heading off to see the latest Damien Chazelle film with the love of your life?

Now that I was single my diary had really opened up, as had the Pandora's box full of my fears about myself and . . . everything. Suddenly there was room to think about all the other things that were seriously wrong, piling on top of each other like some grim grief sundae. The end of my relationship might have pulled the rug out from under me, but it turned out that rug had been unravelling for some time.

Recently some close friends of mine, Ash and Dan, told me of an interview they'd listened to which touched on the loss of confidence that can occur in your forties or fifties. Dan, who was mid-career-change, generally questioning his life choices and in somewhat of a funk, turned to his younger partner and said, 'Maybe that's what I'm going through – a midlife crisis?' Ash lowered his sunglasses and replied dryly, 'Do you think?'

I totally get Dan's surprise. It took me a while to acknowledge what all the evidence pointed to in my own case, and like him it came as a relief when I did. After all, this was completely normal at my age. Naturally I was questioning my job and my place in the world. That would be easy to fix: worst-case scenario, I could just do the Camino walk and, screw it, get a facelift.

Tragically, though, it turned out that Dan was not feeling tired and depressed because of a clichéd psychological crisis. Weeks later he was diagnosed with acute myeloid leukemia (mercifully, he's now doing so well that we've taken to calling him 'Super Dan'). Sometimes, even though it swims and quacks and has feathers, it isn't a duck after all.

I didn't have cancer. Like many others before me I'd reached the middle (hopefully) of my life and was wondering what it's all about, asking myself, How am I going to spend the rest of my years? That's not necessarily confined to middle age, either; I recently spoke to a thirty-year-old who said he felt that he'd already had at least two crises, and god knows, this didn't feel like my first time at the existential-angst rodeo. But it certainly felt like I was peaking. I didn't feel good about *anything*.

In retrospect, the trigger had been pulled by my brother's death. I remember, days after his funeral, feeling so grateful to be back home but also, suddenly and for the first time, terrified of dying. Your parents are meant to shuffle off before you, and, horrible though it is, close friends dying too young feels random enough for you to go on believing that your roulette number is unlikely to come up, but there's something about a sibling dying – even one who's twelve years older – that makes you hear the reaper's scythe tapping at the window.

My death no longer seemed so completely ridiculous. It's probably an odd parallel to draw, but when you haven't had sex for a while, or ever, the idea of it seems preposterous. You might as well tell a friend that you're considering opening a microbrewery with a pixie. It's the very humanness of it, the bodily fluids and vulnerability, that removes it from the neatness of most of our lives. And death, like that potentially life-giving act, has its own messiness and seems inconceivable – until it doesn't.

When Niall died I was in a relationship; now that I was single, I felt like a skinned animal. I was in a play where some unnameable terror pervades every scene. Hang on a minute, I thought, this isn't supposed to happen. I'm a white, heterosexual, non-disabled, ciswoman with a lot going for her – am I going to have to cope with sounding self-indulgent and whiney as well? This so isn't fair!

Maybe because I'm all those things that was my other problem. I really had always naively trusted that it would all work out in the end. We're hardwired to believe in happy endings, so I just thought that, regardless of my history, ultimately everything would be great! The randomness of existence didn't apply to me. What on earth was I basing this on? Did I think life was like a movie? (Yes, if all my film references are anything to go by.) Which one? *Toy Story*? Did I think I was going to be rescued by an animated toy cowboy voiced by Tom Hanks?

I'd managed to ignore all the evidence. My father died completely estranged from his children and had led a life of thwarted dreams. My mother's life was a litany of health problems and frustrations at the hands of a chauvinist husband, and my brother had died a painful death too young. Did I think these were all exceptions to the rule? As for all the people who've experienced war, natural disasters and a whole host of other tragedies, I guess I thought they just hadn't tried hard enough to turn their frowns upside down.

I'm not the only person who's a complete idiot. Jonathan Rauch's *The Happiness Curve* describes how our youthful optimism slowly evaporates as we enter middle age until it picks up again in our fifties (I'm still waiting for that to happen). The reason is that we've been given false ideas about what makes us content. People often arrive in their forties with a family, a home and a successful career only to realise that something is missing.

I'd been wondering about the direction my career might take for some time. Actually, when hadn't I? (If I'd married stand-up comedy, we'd have had many trial separations by now, each ending with me sheepishly coming back because nobody else would have me.) I was becoming more aware of the state of my livelihood at unexpected times, such as in my local bottle shop, a place I generally associate with unbridled joy. As I went to buy my pinot noir, the man behind the counter said, 'Judith . . .?' I said, 'Lucy,' and he said, 'Oh yeah, what happened? Are you still around? Do you even do comedy anymore?' Sadly, I actually tried to tell him what I'd been doing for the past few years, in an effort to prove that I could still make people laugh for a living. Then I gave up and just bought a lot more alcohol, along with a ton of beef jerky, which really showed that I'd lost the will to live.

When my brother was sick, I was working on a show for the ABC called *Judith Lucy is All Woman*. It was about being a woman (and a man) in Australia today, and if it had a point it was that gender stereotypes suck. Filming was hard work but it's always incredible to be paid to do what I love doing the most: interviewing others and hearing how they make sense of life. Unfortunately, Niall entered his last days during post-production, and taking time away from him to give notes on the latest edit was awful for me and for the line producer, who had to keep reminding me we had to meet a deadline (a particularly loaded word at the time).

It turned into one of those projects where everything seemed hard. I wasn't the only person dealing with painful personal stuff, and most of the core production team barely crawled over the finish line. I may never watch that series again. I'm proud of some of what we did, like getting an extraordinary collection of female singers together to perform a new version of 'I am Woman', but when one reviewer said that the series was a wasted opportunity, I had to admit they might be right. The show didn't strike a chord with the viewing audience, and in retrospect I hadn't been honest enough in it.

When I made a series about spirituality I put myself on the line, which meant that despite the enormity of the topic, the show had direction and coherence, based in the truth of my own life. I didn't do the same with *All Woman*: I wanted it to be a show that appealed to people who didn't think of themselves as feminists but who might be inspired to reconsider. It was well intentioned, but so are a lot of shit things. Not only was my plan a little patronising, but how could I be genuine about the struggles of women on camera when there was so much about my own attitudes to gender that I hadn't admitted to or even interrogated properly? It's a pity I didn't understand that at the time, because such interrogation might have made for some interesting television.

I'd hoped my career might be headed towards more regular TV work, but around the time of *All Woman* I also

IS IT A DUCK?

learnt that a job I'd been pinning my hopes on wasn't going to happen. For over a year it'd looked like film critic Jason Di Rosso and I were going to take over from the much loved David Stratton and Margaret Pomeranz on *At the Movies*, with their blessing. It seemed that I was going to get what I'd been increasingly craving: job security and a steady income doing something I love, watching and reviewing movies. No more touring or mining my life for gags. They were very big shoes to fill but I was keen to give it a crack.

Somewhere along the way, though, the ABC changed their mind. Worse than losing this particular gig was the realisation that the network I'd always assumed would be there for me, and where I'd worked on and off since I was twenty-five, didn't feel quite the same way so that safety net was definitely gone. I know I was lucky to have ever had it but it felt like another door shutting.

And then the phone just stopped ringing. No one gives you any warning about this. No one knocks on your door and says, 'You know how things have been pretty good for the past twenty-five years? That's all about to end. Actually, I guess we should've told you that sooner so you could have saved some money and made some plans. Whoops.'

It wasn't that I'd arrogantly assumed my career would go on forever – somehow, I just chose not to think about it, or plan for my future in any way. It's hard to know whether this was stupidity, self-sabotage or an unconscious belief that a man would solve everything. I suspect it was all three. What a terrific three-way bet! Back those racehorses, everyone, you simply can't lose! I now also see that I didn't value my future enough to actually invest in it. I seemed to think that would only be worth doing when I was in a relationship.

Ironically, the show *Disappointments* that Scotty and I performed turned out to be very successful. As Kev said, 'You've gone beyond both of your fan bases, it's like you've tapped into the *Menopause the Musical* audience.' This made the two of us both happy and sad. The downside for me was that in spending so much time with Scotty I was aware of every single offer she was getting, while it felt like I was getting none. I became convinced that, apart from performing live (and thank god for that), my career was really in the shitter.

The words of the late, great comedian Lynda Gibson kept ringing in my ears: 'Comedy is a young person's game.' Scotty was clearly the exception that proved the rule, and this was confirmed when I went to a yearly comedy lunch organised by Jack Levi. Some of you may remember that his character Elliot Goblet was once a household name. There were many familiar faces around the table but hardly any of them were making a living from comedy anymore. Corporate gigs had dried up because businesses were only interested in young people who were on television and commercial radio. One gentleman told me that he was now forced to MC weddings for a pittance. The future seemed pretty grim.

IS IT A DUCK?

All of this amplified the sense of uselessness I often felt about what I did for a living. Was I really put on this planet to tell stories about passing out in yet another public toilet while the Amazon rainforest was on fire? Shouldn't I be helping people in Africa or chaining myself to Parliament House to protest our treatment of refugees and First Nations Peoples? WHAT WAS I DOING WITH MY LIFE?

This was the other thing I'd been avoiding: you know, the world. Every generation feels that it's living in scary times. We gen Xers were all terrified of nuclear war when we were kids but that was somehow more comprehensible than the idea that we're killing the whole planet. At least the bomb-dropping thing always seemed like it could be avoided: 'Come on guys, let's pour a whiskey, light a cigar and just nut this shit out.' Climate change involves getting your head around almost inconceivable consequences and valuing the long term over the short. Far better to mine, frack and be merry.

It astonishes me that, as a species, we're still around. Even rats in a science experiment seem to have the ability to learn from their mistakes, but not us. I'm sure we'll soon have sex robots and the technology to download our consciousness, which is terrific, but none of that will mean much when we're living in Cormac McCarthy's *The Road*. It's all so overwhelming; simpler to watch Netflix and make another wellness smoothie with some almond milk and a couple of Endone.

I'm old enough to remember when people trusted: the Church, doctors, the police force, banks and the TV news.

Admittedly, that trust was often misplaced. When we kids went to the doctor he'd offer us a lollipop while he lit up another cigarette. I'm actually surprised he didn't say, 'Mrs Lucy, can I offer you a line?' I don't know that anyone ever trusted politicians, but we at least had the illusion that voting mattered and that the world wasn't entirely riddled with corruption.

I wish there was some rationale to the awfulness. Really, I'd start believing in conspiracy theories and some overarching evil plan involving Bill Gates, vaccination and the 5G network, but I don't think humans are capable of being that smart and organised. If Taylor Swift actually *was* the high priestess of the Church of Satan, it would make her so much more interesting. Instead I think we're largely motivated by what's in front of us and what we can get right now. That's right, we're all Shane Warne.

What the fuck could I do about all of this? Every day, all I did was ask myself questions, because I was desperate for some sort of quick-fix answer. I liked the idea of a dramatic change and wondered if I should go overseas as a volunteer. What about a different job, something that could pay the bills while I devoted the rest of my time to an important cause?

I thought very seriously about becoming a celebrant as a way to earn a living that freed up some time. After the Marriage Equality Bill was passed some friends suggested that I should not only start marrying and burying people, but specialise in gay weddings. (To be honest, this idea is still very appealing, so if this turkey ever gets published, you're reading it and considering tying the knot, check my Facebook page. It could be what I'm doing now.)

I thought about joining a church – I hadn't rediscovered Jesus but was still deeply interested in spirituality, and maybe what I needed was a community. I had buddies, but was that enough? Why didn't I know my neighbours? I remembered one block of flats I lived in where I was the only tenant who didn't attend the Christmas drinks – I watched the whole thing behind my closed blinds and wondered what was wrong with me. (Mind you, the only interaction I ever had with one downstairs neighbour in that place was when she opened the door as I walked past and said, 'You're an animal.' I think I may have been a little loud.) Did I hate people? What did I really care about? My god, should I move back TO PERTH?

No, that was a bridge too far although when I returned for my old best friend Michelle's fiftieth I did find myself envying how many close relationships she had in her life: her husband and two children, her mother and one of her brothers (two relatives I no longer had), his partner and offspring. Growing up, these people had been my second family, shouldn't I see them more often? Jan and most of my birth relatives live in Perth, including Mum's sister, Paddy. I didn't have any of that in Melbourne. I remember someone my age who'd also left Perth long ago reflecting on what a huge decision it is to move away voluntarily from your parents and the place you grew up. He felt that your new life had to have a hell of a lot going for it to make up for missing out on time with your mum and dad as they aged, along with not really knowing your extended family. I'd made the decision to leave Perth so effortlessly but now I wondered what was keeping my life tethered in Melbourne.

In the end, I did something truly momentous: I cleaned my flat. I went through every room and threw a lot of stuff out. It took me so long that I really needed to start a second clean as soon as I finished (I don't live in a mansion, I'm just slow). On reflection, I was glad I hadn't done anything more dramatic – on some level I must have known I was in no state to make big changes. I'll never forget deciding to go overseas (maybe forever!) after learning I was adopted: it was an unmitigated disaster. This time, just sitting with my uncertainty, and doing little things like cleaning and setting up a new bank account to save some money made me feel like I was getting some control back. These tiny decisions were really all I was capable of, but I started to think that if I just kept putting one foot in front of the other I might eventually feel better about my life.

Don't panic, Australia! I also concluded that I'd be crazy to walk away from comedy when I've devoted over thirty years to it and I'm not shit. Comedy had afforded me the opportunity to write books and do TV series in the past, and these hadn't just been about throwing up on my own underpants – maybe I could continue to explore issues along with writing jokes? After all, I'd been on this journey for some time.

IS IT A DUCK?

Sure, for years I *had* just told hilarious, vomit-related anecdotes, but at thirty-six, when I was fired from my high-paying commercial radio job, I realised that it was time to stop stumbling along and start trying to work on projects I was passionate about. Being paid to be funny just wasn't enough for me anymore. Losing my job had been pretty humiliating but no more so than the kind of work I'd been doing on air, which amounted to telling gags in between Britney Spears tracks and McDonald's giveaways. I finally understood that I didn't mind failing if it was at something I actually cared about.

My first venture after that was writing *The Lucy Family Alphabet*, and not long after that I did the series on spirituality. I'd always tried to make my live shows be about more than just jokes (not that there's anything wrong with just jokes, by the way) but they were still the priority. Now I was doing work where the punchlines were the tools I used to explore anything from family dynamics to religion, and it was a real turning point.

Apparently the jig wasn't completely up when it came to my career. The phone did start ringing again, with some TV work along with other interesting offers, everything from acting in a sitcom to appearing in a feminist documentary about an older woman embarking on a career in porn. I started going to opening nights and parties. Had I not been receiving these invitations before, or was the real difference that I was now saying yes to them?

When I looked around at my social network and the communities I was a part of in Melbourne I saw that I was surrounded by possibilities. In fact, what struck me was how used I'd got to saying no, especially when asked to do something new or out of my comfort zone. This had started even before I was with Mr Rabbit. Most days, what I looked forward to – and this was definitely the case when I was in a relationship – was going home and shutting the door. If my night also happened to involve a glass of wine or two and an episode or five of a favourite TV series, so much the better. What was I *doing*? Was I going to say on my deathbed, 'I didn't drink enough wine and I never got through all of *Grey's Anatomy*. Oh god, why didn't I make time for more television? I never even started *Suits*.'

I also realised that it had been a very long time since someone had said, 'How are you?' and I'd replied, 'Great.' Or even 'Good.' 'Alright' was what I generally said. That was understandable when I was dealing with a crisis, but when I wasn't, why was I living this half-life? How long had that been going on? Years, I admitted.

While I'd done some interesting projects, and always been fortunate in my friends, for longer than I could remember my life had revolved around work – the stress that went with it and then dulling my senses with TV, booze, dope or more often a combination of all three. I reached a point where I only got trashed with other people, but I still needed something to take the edge off when I was on my own, even if it was just bingeing on *The Good Fight*.

IS IT A DUCK?

Yoga, meditation and a lot of reading about spirituality, Buddhism in particular, had helped, but I felt like I was stuck on some sort of wheel (samsara, as the Buddhists would say). There were moments of contentment and achievement but I always came undone when there were family dramas or another broken heart. I was better at it, sure (there was definitely more downward dog than just face-down in the gutter these days). But the dynamic hadn't changed and a lot of it revolved around a man – being with one, wanting to be with one, or pretending that I was fine not being with one. I wasn't as much of a halfwit as I'd been in my twenties but I wasn't different enough either. I felt so *stuck*.

Now, without Mr R, I just couldn't kid myself anymore. None of the distractions I'd used were working. I began to see that I viewed so much of my life as a chore: work, obviously, but also phone calls and the upkeep that every relationship needs. I love spending time with people but somewhere along the way it had become an obligation, a box that I grudgingly ticked. Everything was just a precursor to locking the door, because then I wouldn't feel uncomfortable or tense. I wouldn't be overthinking everything I said and did, it would just be me (and sometimes a partner) with an episode of *Law and Order* and a glass of wine and the absence of worry. Without realising it, this was what I seemed to be living for, this totally false idea of safety.

But of course, we're never safe, and life had shown me this many times. I remember a yoga teacher saying that even if you lock your door, whatever you're trying to hide from will find you; I felt like it hadn't just discovered where I lived but blown my door off its hinges. It was nifty to tell myself it was a midlife crisis, but these were issues I'd been dealing with most of my adult life. Oh fuck, had I really just been trying to outrun myself?

My feelings of uneasiness about comedy not being worthwhile were really about *me* not being worthwhile. I'd been trying to outrun these doubts, which for years I'd hoped would be assuaged by men, who only ended up amplifying that feeling. I couldn't keep living like this, could I?

I also began to see that I'd known I had to change for a long time but somehow denied it. However unhappy I'd been, at least I knew that feeling – it was awful but it was familiar. Unhappy was, in a way, me. What would I be without it? And trying to change – *really* change – is fucking hard.

Where do you even start?

PART THREE
Trying

9

One Hot Cunt

Sorting the Body Stuff Out

The good news was that I'd worked out what my issues were! The bad news was that they appeared to be ME and EVERYTHING!

Changing that was certainly going to keep me busy. At least I knew that doing *something* – even trying to – was way better than doing nothing. I actually didn't even feel that I had a choice; there's only so much self-loathing a girl can take.

First, I doubled down on being a funny lady. I didn't just stick with comedy, it became the very expression of and sometimes vehicle for my transition. I didn't grasp it until I was well into the process, but writing and performing *Judith Lucy versus Men* turned out to be the starting point for overhauling my life, and that was followed by the much more obvious attempt at doing so in the podcast series,

Judith Lucy Overwhelmed and Dying. I'm sure that one day I'll tire of exploiting my personal struggles for cash, but I'm not there yet, baby, so strap in.

I'd known *Versus* was going to be a re-examination of my past with men of course, but I didn't expect it to reveal just how much I'd sought their affirmation, nor what I'd put up with to get it. The show helped me recognise that despite the nightly audience vote that I continue looking for Mr Right, I didn't want to live like that anymore. I also knew that this was just the beginning. I'm not sure what was more difficult, trying different approaches to my problems or letting go of the old ones.

That tour wasn't just a starting point for change, it was also responsible for the most mystifying message that has ever been passed on to me, in this case by an usher. A young gay woman had said that the show made her want to finger me in the arsehole. The usher then added, 'And she was really pretty.' Who knew what the future had in store? What did I want that future to look like? Did my rectum require fingering by an attractive lesbian? I didn't have a clue. All I knew was that I didn't want to dwell on wasted time. I've never seen the point in that. *Je ne regrette rien*. I actually *regrette* plenty but I wasn't the only person who wore stirrup pants in the eighties and there was nothing I could do about that.

I knew I wanted not just to make peace with aging but embrace it, and that society wasn't going to help me with that. It wasn't going to help a lady in her fifties feel great about her sexuality, either. Those were just the amuse-bouches, though; main course was believing that my life was worthwhile. More than anything, I needed to feel that I was playing even a small part in making things a bit less shit on the planet. I also knew that if I was grappling with everything from rising sea levels to personal anguish, so were a lot of people, and this inspired the podcast series.

I figured that in trying to work some of this stuff out, I might help a few other humans along the way, or at least make them feel relieved they're not me. *Overwhelmed and Dying* covered everything from life purpose to dating, refugees to grassroots movements, climate change to death. I went swimming in freezing-cold water and did sex therapy and got to speak to everyone from a nun who'd just left the convent to Tim Winton. The very act of making the podcast confirmed that comedy and I still had a way to go on our merry dance. I loved every minute of it.

A lot of people are, like me, at their best when doing work that means something to them, but I also need to have a question to answer. In *The Lucy Family Alphabet*, for instance, I was looking at whether or not I hated my parents. (No, surprisingly, was the answer.) Over time I've discovered that this means I have to be as honest as possible. (Look out, I'm turning into Brené Brown.) And being honest means you have to make yourself vulnerable. Also, if you don't disappear up your own arsehole, this is the way to make your quest universal. I put myself through shit so that both the audience and I hopefully get a few answers.

The podcast was a godsend: it got me back out into the world, experimenting with ideas on how to live my life and, more importantly, connecting with people who were prepared to answer my openness with their own. It's amazing what folks will tell you if you just ask them and actually listen to their answer. I hope that those who listened to the show got even a fraction of what I did out of making it. The series got me a lot further than if I'd been trying to nut this stuff out on my own. Plus I got paid (sort of, it *was* the ABC) so it was a real win-win.

The journey began with the physical. Episodes two and three were called 'A Lesson My Arse Taught Me' and 'Hanging up My Vagina'. I know, don't feel bad, I'm a professional writer who just has a gift when it comes to language.

I've always been intrigued by the idea of 'wellness'. Maybe that's because Mum was taking vitamins and all sorts of herbal remedies years before it became fashionable. She tried acupuncture and saw naturopaths for her various maladies, but I think what she really needed was a different life. The spectre of sickness constantly hung over me too. Ann Lucy was very overprotective and I was always the kid who wasn't allowed to play sport, or had too many layers of underwear on so I wouldn't 'catch pneumonia and die'.

Anyone would have thought we were in a war zone, there were so many activities that could result in death: catching the bus, riding a bike, going on a Ferris wheel, and of course eating cheese (I was supposedly allergic to dairy). I'm pretty sure I was actually fairly robust but I'll never know, since my upbringing had a slight touch of the Munchausen-by-proxy feel to it.

While it seems obvious that Mum's control of me was a way of making up for the lack of authority she had over her own life, I suspect that my being a girl played into it as well. I'm not too sure how women wound up being labelled the weaker sex when you consider the incredible acts our bodies are capable of, but my mother certainly bought into the idea that I was 'delicate'. To be fair, she had no real idea what was swimming around in my gene pool, and that must have played a part too. And initially, at least, she would've been very aware that another mother had entrusted her with her child.

Not that long ago, as part of my half-hearted quest to find out who my birth father is, I discovered that in the first few weeks of my adoption, Mum went so far as to have me admitted to hospital for forty-eight hours for observation. There was nothing wrong with me but the documents refer to Mum being 'fussy' and needing reassurance – I don't think that feeling left her until I turned eighteen. A switch definitely got flicked in Ann Lucy's head at that point. I could have said, 'Mum, I've decided to let my axe-throwing boyfriend with the DTs put an apple on my head and use it as target practice,' and I'm pretty confident that she would have said, 'Wonderful! Bring it home with you and we'll make some granola!'

Until then, though, my health was a constant concern, or maybe she was just fucking our family GP and that's why we seemed to be in his waiting room almost every other week.

So I inherited a pretty exaggerated fear of illness from Ann Lucy. I too wound up taking copious vitamins as an adult and was always worried about sore throats turning into colds and infections. Performing while ill isn't much fun and my touring schedule could be pretty gruelling, but on later tours I ended up living like a cloistered nun, never going out after the show or having any fun – and yet I still got sick, so I might as well have been shelving ketamine and banging sailors.

Another enlightening piece of information from my early hospital visit was that I had 'mild bowel problems'. That could explain why I was so obsessed with my arse and irritable bowel syndrome in later years. I have no idea if that's what I actually had as an adult, but for a long time I was preoccupied with being bloated and having constipation. It's probably no coincidence that Ann Lucy was also a laxative addict but I know many ladies who are obsessed with this region of their body. We're more complicated down there because our junk isn't hanging outside but has to share the space with our organs of digestion and elimination. It's all tied up with eating, diet and body image, so no wonder our guts are a loaded issue.

A couple of years ago I decided I was going to do whatever it took to get 'better'. I tried the FODMAP diet, I was tested for allergies, I gave my doctor stool samples, I tried breath analysis, I even saw an ayurvedic doctor, who, on top of many other things, injected a type of ghee into my rectum. This was done on four separate occasions, after which I had to 'hold in' for a certain amount of time. (Usually I was doing this gripping while on a tram. If you want to know the definition of concentration, I would say it's trying to hold your sphincter shut on public transport so that you don't release a mixture of oil and faeces. If the number 78 tram is anything to go by, not everyone wins that battle.) I will never eat butter chicken again.

None of these remedies worked. Out of sheer desperation I tried hypnotherapy, which at least made me realise that in my case the culprit was probably stress. If I could deal with that and generally look after my health, it would probably make a big difference. It also made me understand that what I really needed to do was STOP THINKING ABOUT IT.

Stress management and trying to live a reasonably healthy life turned things around. I also stopped beating myself up if I went out for a couple of drinks after a show, and no longer got a taxi to ICU if I had a tickle at the back of my throat. When I consider what I've put my body through over the years, I think it's incredible I haven't just burst into flames, or needed to be buried under layers of concrete thanks to my toxicity levels, yet instead of being thankful for that I was fixated on not feeling amazing one hundred per cent of the time. In my fifties, I actually started to dwell on all the stuff my body could do instead of what it couldn't, and that was a genuine breakthrough for me.

For the podcast, I wanted to talk to someone who could give this sort of practical advice about the best way to deal with time and its effects on us physically and mentally. I interviewed scientist Dr Jen Martin, who I'd been listening to on community radio station RRR for years. She had shed light on numerous topics for me as a listener and she was just as delightful and informative in person. Jen talked about the Blue Zones, the areas in the world where people live ridiculously long and healthy lives. There are a number of reasons for this: the inhabitants move (it doesn't have to be a gym workout, but keeping active is essential); they have a mainly plant-based diet; they only eat until they're eighty per cent full; they have a reason for getting out of bed in the morning; they are close to their families; they're involved with their community; they have a way of dealing with stress; and (terrific news) they have a moderate wine intake. The theory behind stopping eating before you're completely full is that it combats inflammation in the body, which is a leading cause of disease. I like eating and drinking until I can feel the contents of my stomach at the back of my throat, but it's something to work towards (Balaclava, Melbourne, isn't quite Okinawa, Japan, but I'm having a go).

None of this was about appearance or Instagram-worthiness and it all seemed pretty sensible. Admittedly, Dr Saul Newman disputed the Blue Zones theory while we were still making the podcast. He said that many of the places mentioned didn't keep accurate records, and in some cases people had simply lied about their age, but others claim that he's been selective with the data to prove his point. In the end we thought, Fuck it, it still seems like pretty good advice.

Another tip Jen gave was about the significance of new memories. If you want to slow time down, break some habits. Don't go to the same cafe every day or eat the same food. Go on a holiday, listen to some new music, talk to someone different. To put this a bit more bluntly, don't start nailing down your coffin lid when you're still years away from dying. A neighbour's mother, on hearing I was about to turn forty, said to me, 'I'm seventy-eight. I'd give anything to be your age again.' I don't want to look back at my fifties when I'm eighty and regret that I'd already started drinking Bovril and wearing slacks.

In this same episode of the podcast I also interviewed Shae Graham, the first woman to represent Australia in wheelchair rugby, or murderball. Shae was in an accident when she was eighteen and has been in a wheelchair ever since. Hearing about the gruelling mental and physical rehabilitation she went through is enough to put anyone's gripes about their chunky thighs to bed, although Shae admitted that she too still has those comparatively trivial moments of insecurity from time to time. Ultimately, though, she is blown away by her body's resilience and has an incredible appreciation for the simplest of activities that many of us take for granted. Like walking: she marvels at what that demands from both the brain and the body. I asked her what she thought of people obsessing over their weight and she ended by saying, 'I just think everyone should eat cake and be happy.' I still might put that on a T-shirt.

Some of the activities I tried for the podcast I would've done anyway, but that doesn't include swimming at seven am at Brighton Beach with the Icebergers club. This is a group of people who, every day, come rain or shine, do laps in the ocean some time between dawn and early morning. I went out with eighty-year-old Jan and Alison, somewhere in her sixties. I say 'swim' but I really just walked in up to my neck, screamed and ran straight out to the steam room. I'd read that the icy water can bring on a heart attack, and there's only so much suffering I'm prepared to do for my art.

I wish I'd taken a microphone into the steam room, because I was extremely grateful to the woman who told me I wasn't being a wimp, I'd picked the coldest month of the year to plunge into the Pacific. And I wanted to make a pass at the old guy who told me I should keep coming because these morning swims were the best hangover cure ever.

According to the Icebergers website, swimming regularly in the ocean improves mental and physical wellbeing. I have no interest in freezing my nipples off on a regular basis, so I'll never know about that but I could certainly see the benefits of watching the sun rise above the ocean. Jan and Alison did berate me for not sticking around for coffee, because that's also part of the experience apparently. That seemed to me what really keeps these people young: being out in nature and part of a community. Alison and

Jan didn't seem fussed about getting older. Alison thought she looked better now because she was happier, one of the reasons for this, being that she 'finds joy in little moments'.

Yoga is my salvation. I know I've banged on about it already, but it was the thing that got me through the break-up, once I'd stopped crying and returned to a decent practice. I'm stronger and fitter now than I've ever been. Admittedly I'm coming from a low bar, but that's the beauty of doing no exercise whatsoever in your twenties and thirties. I love that feeling of being fit and I want to appreciate it because I know it won't last. Recently, I was doing something in Pilates next to a much older woman and it made me aware that I should enjoy everything I'm currently physically capable of. I thought about what a privilege it is just to be able to move.

Sometimes when I'm walking along on a sunny day, I feel completely in my body and am so grateful to it. I even tell it that. I know how that sounds (I haven't ended up with a cat, so I may as well chat to my hamstrings) but when I finish a yoga practice, I always thank my body now. It still does pretty much everything I ask it to and more. I feel very silly when I consider how long it took me to realise how lucky this makes me.

These days I really do try not to dwell on aches and wrinkles and whatever the hell it is that still comes out of my vagina occasionally and looks like it's straight from a tar factory. A friend says it's my uterus in its death throes, but it's just all part of my body changing, and when I'm not torturing myself with thoughts of my lost allure I feel pretty good in this skin of mine.

But why limit myself to yoga? Last year, at fifty-one, I learnt how to ride a bike. Initially, it was going to be for my curtain call for *Judith Lucy versus Men* because for some unknown reason, every boyfriend I've ever had has insisted they would teach me to ride and none of them did, so I thought it might make a nice point at the end of the show. (But I had to drop it because negotiating the different stage sizes while touring demanded the riding skills of a circus clown.) I have no idea why boyfriends always made this offer, I never asked them and it always struck me as odd that none of them ever wanted to teach me how to swim – something that could potentially save my life one day. If the ship goes down, I'm not going to be pedalling to shore.

I can't fuck a Malvern Star, though. What about that part of my physicality? Being single was one thing but, menopause be damned, I wasn't going to say goodbye to being a sexual person. I don't ever want to do that. In fact, now that I'm single, I really want to take the time to explore my desires because I don't have to worry about pleasing anyone else. It makes me furious that, after a certain age, women simply aren't seen as being capable of or interested in passion and sensuality anymore. I intend to fight that one kicking and screaming.

About five years ago I had some botox injected into my G spot for the *All Woman* TV show. It was the episode where we looked at cosmetic procedures – I didn't want botulism injected into my face, so when I heard that this was another option I thought it might make for some interesting television. (They haven't found an excuse to put it up your anus yet, but when they do I'll be there!) It all seemed like a great idea until I was lying on my back with a camera pointed at my clacker. The joke really was on me, as I've since read that the G spot is probably a myth.

This revelation is part of some very recent research done on the clitoris. Unsurprisingly, male doctors haven't been that interested in the part of the body responsible for the female orgasm. It turns out that the clitoris extends underneath the pubic bone and wraps around the vaginal opening. It apparently looks like an orchid. I'm now going to consider my vulva as a beautiful terrarium. I may even put some lichen, a pine cone and a miniature frog down there. I might even try a shipwreck. But now I know why the injection made no difference: all it did was make a tiny part of my vagina wrinkle-free. For three months a small portion of my canal looked like Reese Witherspoon's forehead. The doctor who gave me the injection said that some male doctors wouldn't give it to women over forty because they didn't see the point – the botox is meant to enhance your pleasure and, as far as they were concerned, women that age were now getting that only from doing craft.

I was thinking about a lot more than felt-making after Mr Rabbit and I broke up. I've mentioned that I masturbated like a motherfucker. Grief had often made me want to get my rocks off. I'm sure a lot of people pick up at funerals; it's the combination of wanting something physical to distract you along with the desire to connect with life in a very primal way. Sick of my own fantasies, one night I actually put 'free porn' into my search engine for the first time ever. Had I been missing out! Oh semen! When are we just going to start putting it in public fountains? I also put in 'submissive women'. As a feminist I always struggle to admit this, but my fantasies are just really lazy. I like a scenario where I don't have to do any of the work, I just lie there passively and orgasm a lot.

I was having dinner with a friend recently and we both admitted that we didn't think we'd had that much good sex. I've had fun and enjoyed the intimacy, but really great, toe-curling fornication? That happened with just one guy – the acrobat. No one else has even suggested anything remotely interesting.

My friend asked me if I'd ever faked an orgasm, and if memory serves it was just the once, when I realised it was the only way I was going to get this heaving gent off of me. I haven't otherwise utilised my acting skills for the sake of someone's ego, and frankly, few men have seemed that bothered about my coming or not. Virtually no one has ever said to me, 'Now what can I do for you?' I've never been terribly good at telling them, either. Partly because I haven't had the confidence, but also because I just can't be bothered. If I need to get a manual out and explain how everything works, I'd rather just have another drink and do a bit of gusset-typing once they've gone.

None of this indicated that I was living my best sexual life. Left to my own devices I can certainly get the job done but I've never run a bath, poured a glass of wine and just had some me-time. I generally just get stoned, get the vibrator out, lie on the couch and think, No wait, we shouldn't do this, I can't . . . stop what are you doing? I said no . . . And then in no time at all I'm done and back watching Netflix.

Sex with another person can obviously be very complicated but why had I never really taken the time to work out what I needed or wanted? We still seem to be in uncharted waters when it comes to female desire. Was Submissive Woman, a male fantasy, the best I could do? On some level, I thought spending time on my own pleasure just wasn't worthwhile and yet the planet revolves around male enjoyment in that area. Why am I trying to work this stuff out only now? I'm a walking cliché. Soon I'm going to go to Greece and start flirting with Tom Conti.

Still, better late than never, I suppose. I knew sex had to be more than a quick orgasm between episodes of *Ozark* so I went exploring. Not long after my last relationship ended, I joined the mailing list of a sensuality store for women called Passionfruit, which, on top of selling all sorts of toys and lingerie, also offers classes and lectures. So off I went to a talk given by a dominatrix. If the comedy fell over, I'd need a backup plan and I look incredible in rubber. The truth was, I wanted to hear about a world where chicks are completely in charge.

There were couples at the lecture and some young women, but inevitably there were two much older men on their own, and part of me wanted to say, 'What are you perverts doing here? She's not going to be giving demonstrations.' And indeed, there was nothing remotely titillating about the talk; it was more a history of the art of BDSM and this particular woman's journey. I found it fascinating because it was so completely removed from my own experience. I even toyed with the idea of exploring it more, attracted by the power these women wield and their bravery in living outside societal norms but, on reflection, while I applaud these ladies and their dress sense, I conceded that it wasn't for me. I had a feeling that seeing a man in a nappy was not what I needed right then ... or ever. Still, I bought a vibrator and wrote down the Katherine Mansfield quote the lecturer had written on the white board: 'Risk! Risk anything! Care no more for the opinions of others, for those voices. Do the hardest thing on earth for you. Act for yourself. Face the truth.'

I would think of this quote about a year later, when I went to the screening of a documentary I'd taken part in, *Morgana*. I'd met the titular protagonist during the *All Woman* series and so knew some of the story that was explored in the film. We're a similar age and the director wanted me to talk about my feelings on aging and sex. Morgana had been in a loveless marriage and at age fifty reinvented herself as a feminist erotic filmmaker. She hasn't had an easy time of it and has had to deal with mental health issues as well, but she's come to live by the idea of not caring what others think, and while I suspect neither bondage nor porn are the answer for me, having the courage to explore my own truth is. My sexuality and, what the hell, my life, are still full of possibilities.

Another concept I wanted to explore was the cuddle party, so I took myself off to one with a camera crew. (That's how I attend everything from colonoscopies to funerals. This particular venture was one of my 'Wellness Warrior' segments for the ABC TV show *The Weekly*.) A cuddle party involves a group of people getting together and, you guessed it, cuddling. Much time is devoted to laying down the rules and there's a very strong emphasis on consent. The one I attended was mainly younger people, with a number identifying as non-binary.

I liked the idea of experiencing affection without sex and I can see that if touch is your thing then these parties might work, but I spent most of the hour feeling like someone was running their nails down a blackboard made of writhing rat babies. I'm simply not good with strangers touching me. Again, there were a couple of older men (one was a fan!) and if they'd so much as brushed my pinkie toe I would have had to amputate the leg. One of them even told me he ran 'sex parties' in the same space, but added that it 'probably wasn't my jam'. Correct. Still, most of the people I met weren't sleazy but warm. I even grudgingly let myself be hugged just before I left. I was glad I went. I wasn't really finding any answers when it came to my sexuality but I was enjoying exploring the question.

My next idea was also inspired by Passionfruit. I opened up one of their emails and it simply read, 'Cunt Portrait'. I remember thinking, Dammit, I'm going to get that done. It was, to be honest, the least confronting option. I wasn't ready for their class, 'Anal Play for Singles and Couples', or 'Going Deeper', which was about deep-throating and fisting. When it comes to new experiences and sexuality, I'm really trying to open myself up, just not all the way to the colon.

I had a visceral response to the cunt portrait invitation, though, and realised I could offset the expense by using it in the *Judith Lucy versus Men* stage show – waste not, want not.

The sculptor, Greg Taylor, did the wall of vulvas at Hobart's MONA gallery, so it wasn't just some dude who thought he could get chicks to dip their bits in plaster as a way of making some extra bucks – it was art! I wanted to embrace my desires, my sexuality and my genitals, and this portrait of my box seemed to tick itself. Even more importantly, it was a way of doing all that without a man. In the typical sense, at least.

And who knew what was going on down there? I'd grabbed a mirror and checked myself out in my late teens, inspired by *Dolly* magazine and later the feminist book *Our Bodies, Ourselves* but since then I'd only had a look when I thought I might have an infection. It goes without saying that I'm appalled, unless you're a transgender person, by the idea of labiaplasty. Is there really no part of the female body we can feel okay about? Apparently not: I've even heard of women getting the fat sucked out of their mons pubis. That reminds me, I've really got to put my perineum on a diet.

The whole experience was quite similar to the vaginal botox injection, in that I managed to give it virtually no thought until I was sitting on some elevated cushions, legs akimbo, with my genitals thirty centimetres from Greg Taylor's face. In the same way that I find myself tuning out when I'm having a pap smear, for the first few minutes I pretended the whole thing wasn't happening. I was just chewing the fat with this eccentric older artist about everything from his growing up on a farm to David Walsh (the owner of MONA) to the fact that he'd only ever slept with three women. And then . . . then I started to feel extremely comfortable. I'd begun with my arms crossed but now those limbs joined my legs in being completely relaxed.

Greg told me that some women had to stop partway through the two-hour process because they felt too tense, but I could have opened a bottle of merlot and a packet of Chicken Twisties and really settled in. I started to enjoy the fact that I was sitting just above this very respectful and slightly awkward man as he stared at my vulva and tried to recreate it in raw clay, which he would then refine and turn into a mold. It would be wrong to say I was aroused by it at all but there was definitely something powerful and exciting about having a man celebrate this part of my body in a totally non-sexual way. I like to think that

I've always been pro-vulva but this experience made me particularly so.

When Greg talked about what a magnificent part of the body it is and how wonderful, as an artist, it was to try to reproduce, I believed him. He told me how some of his subjects burst into tears when they saw their portrait because they'd never seen that part of themselves before. I didn't; I think my first utterance was, 'Greg, I might put my underpants back on.' I didn't just use the sculpture in my last show, I put the image up on a giant screen! A friend said it made her feel better about her own equipment and I was thrilled when a lesbian buddy asked if I'd CGI'd my genitals. I had, that's how we'd made my labia majora look like the sinking *Titanic*.

I have no idea what people took away from my genitals, but for me, in a world full of dicks, it was good to throw a vulva out there in a totally non-erotic way. A man might have made the sculpture but I was completely in charge. The one I toured with is made from resin but I have the very delicate porcelain original in a box (insert own joke) in my wardrobe. I'm not sure what to do with it. Maybe I'll give it to a loved one, or just put it among the bric-a-brac on my bookshelves so that anyone who pokes around can really get to know me. Although, I'm not sure I could do that to my cleaner. Apparently, my portrait is now in MONA too and, for those of you who didn't make it to the show, I'm Judith 155: YOU'RE WELCOME!

Spending this kind of time on myself and my muff was definitely empowering but I hadn't given up on the notion of my sexuality involving someone else. I didn't really know how to do this outside of a relationship or a casual encounter, but dance seemed like a good starting point. Years ago, I met a woman who told me that being single didn't bother her in the least because she's a tango fan, and no matter where she is in the world, she finds a class or club and this sensual dance with a man leaves her feeling satisfied. I'd stored this information away for a rainy, lonely day and also because, dammit, I love to dance!

I partnered with my buddy Ash Flanders, who's not only in a relationship but gay, which seemed entirely right for me. I'd initially thought that doing the class with someone who was actually available might intensify the intimacy of it all, but it turned out that the experience didn't need enhancing. The lesson was . . . excruciating. My eyes locked with Ash's, our hips swayed, and I realised this dance was intimate in a way I hadn't banked on. Finally, our teacher, Dana, said I could stop making eye contact, which certainly helped but I then struggled with following Ash's lead.

Submissive Woman really *was* a fantasy. I like to think I'm a reasonable mover but suddenly I was so self-conscious I couldn't do the most basic step. The whole exercise was meant to be about breathing and connection but I couldn't connect with anything. I needed a drink.

I was struck by my lack of confidence, but then considered that I hadn't been touched by anyone apart from a chiropractor in over two years. I could see how the tango is potentially a great way to reconnect with sexual energy without actually having sex, that you could be sensual with yourself and/or someone else without actually playing hide the salami. The whole idea of being part of a tango community appealed to me because I thought it would be a nice way to wrap my arms around a smokin' guy, but I hadn't understood that it was as much about tapping into something in me, finding my own passion and physical assurance. I'd definitely like to try it again but it's sobering just how quickly that part of you can switch off. If I'd been sexually active I don't think I would have found it so confronting, but as it was, I felt completely vulnerable, and this was with a gay man who's a close friend.

I finally got that drink after the lesson and thought about Dana, who not only teaches tango but works with energies and sees dead people. Yes, those were her exact words. That's one of the problems with making a series, there's never enough time to cover everything, and people are just endlessly bloody fascinating.

Seeing a sex therapist seemed like the next logical step for me. I'd already met Vanessa Muradian filming another wellness segment for *The Weekly* and had really liked her, but we'd hardly used any of the footage. I talked briefly about my break-up with her that first time, and when we spoke again (we actually spoke three times. Here's a tip: don't try to record an interview on a busy street when you have access to an ABC studio) she confirmed that a break-up can butcher your trust and confidence. Vanessa helped me understand that there are other ways of tapping into sensual energy, without feeling so exposed, by pointing out the connection between creativity and sexuality. When we're in a state of flow our mind shuts off, which puts us more completely into the activity we're doing, whether it's writing, performing or sex. I'd never connected those feelings before. Vanessa also talked about a recently widowed woman who'd found her 'expanded, sensual state' by starting to take photographs. That was all very lovely, but I wasn't going to come while taking a beautiful black-and-white shot of a bird.

Then Vanessa did something I wasn't expecting. She asked me to close my eyes and drop into my big toe. Next she told me to move that focus to my clitoris. It was quite a leap and I had to admit that I'd never thought to do that before – something as simple as shifting my awareness so that I could feel that sexual energy. It makes a difference. Seriously, try it. Give it a crack when you're on the tram, or maybe talking to a shop assistant you like the look of. It's subtle, but it does make you remember that you're a sexual being, and can tap into that whenever and wherever you want to. Not only does it put you more in touch with your own body and desires, but it also opens the door to possibility. I know that some women lose interest in sex and are completely happy with that, but that's not me. I still want to explore all the different ways my body can feel, including being turned on even if the only person that involves is me. So, get on board, I'm doing it right now. When you've had enough of that, why not do some Kegel exercises and give your pelvic floor a workout. Hopefully the kilos will just drop off your mons pubis.

I'd tapped into my sensuality; I'd also meditated, danced, posed for an artist and gone to lectures and a cuddle party. It had all been helpful but what about a root?

Many years ago, I had sex with a male escort and, despite getting a routine out of it, very much came to the conclusion that it was too expensive and wholly unremarkable. Still, I was twenty-seven then, and maybe it would be interesting to try it again now that I was in my fifties. There are very few agencies that cater for women, so I went to personal websites. What a mixed bunch! What struck me was how many guys looked like they worked in a bank but obviously thought, I reckon I'm hot enough to screw babes on the side for some filthy lucre. One guy, who'd clearly lied about his age, described his body type as 'athletic to muscular', when the reality was athletic to fucking delusional. I'm not saying there isn't room for all shapes and sizes because of course there is, but the guys didn't seem to feel beholden to the same exacting standards applied to female sex workers.

I spent hours looking over those sites but in the end I just couldn't do it. Part of the problem was that I didn't feel comfortable meeting up with a stranger. I don't remember giving it a second thought when I was younger, and it wasn't like I'd be sharing the experience with the nation as part of the podcast, this was just for me, but I didn't want to put myself in a position with a man where I felt so exposed (I only do that if my naked genitals are going to wind up in an art gallery).

Instead, I went on an introduction date with Adam (not his real name, as he informed me). This is when you hang out, have a drink, and see if you want to have sex later. Adam was not unattractive; the problem was that I paid for the drinks and he didn't ask me a single question. As a friend said afterwards, 'So it was just like one of your normal dates?' I gave him the fifty bucks and couldn't get out of there fast enough. My issue was bigger than this guy being a bit of a dick. Initially, I thought it was because I was now older and more aware of the complexities of paying for sex, but it was deeper than that. I was finally understanding that I didn't want a man to be the solution to my problems. Especially, given my track record, one that involved my bank account.

So there you have it, readers: I learned that it's about taking care of yourself. Partly that means keeping fit and healthy but it's also about much more than that. I didn't get laid but I now know that I can feel sensual and physically confident simply by being more present with the sexual side of myself. I can explore my body and my desires all on my own, and I want to take the time to discover what really floats my boat. A contraption that's been helping me with that is called the Womanizer. The person who recommended it said it was like going home with the sleaziest guy in the bar: you know you shouldn't but it turns out to be the best sex you've ever had. Please get on board, everyone. It works by applying differing degrees of air pressure to the head of the clitoris, and may have you asking why you've ever bothered with anything or anybody that you can't plug in and recharge.

I also came to understand that this isn't just about the physical or sex, it's really about self-worth. Someone who saw *Judith Lucy versus Men* told me that as they were leaving the theatre, they heard someone say, 'Well, how is she going to top that?' referring to my cunt portrait. It's a good question. I finished the show with it because it was my way of claiming my sexuality without a man. The final lines of the piece were: 'I didn't care what [Greg] thought of me, my body, or that part of my body. Obviously, I wasn't sitting there thinking, Am I going to see him again? Is he the one? Finally, and I really do mean finally, it was just all about me. And you know what, fellas? Your loss. Because let's face it, that is one hot cunt.'

10

How Not to be an Arsehole Person

A hot cunt is all well and good but it's not a reason to get out of bed in the morning, unless your labia are on fire.

One of my favourite lines in the movie *Planes, Trains and Automobiles* is when Steve Martin's character turns to John Candy's and says, 'And by the way, when you're telling these little stories? Here's a good idea: have a point.' I needed my life to have a point. I'd made a start but *Overwhelmed and Dying* put my foot on the accelerator. I would encourage everyone to make a podcast although I think that's already happened. Maybe that's because doing these shows enables you to talk to people who might actively avoid you in other situations, like at the butcher's. I really couldn't have asked Buddhist nun Robina Courtin or journalist David Leser about life purpose if we'd been standing next to each other buying mince. They and others helped me explore some deep shit, and one of the themes that emerged was the importance of helping others – connection, dude.

Okay, this wasn't a complete revelation. The social justice aspect of Catholicism is often held up as one of its enduring positives (thank god there's something), so I'd been brought up with the idea of altruism. But once I'd walked away from that religion, the notion had taken a back seat, to be replaced by good times, writing gags, and the self-obsession most of us experience in our early twenties. (Sure, I'm sad about poor people but WHAT AM I GOING TO WEAR TO THE PAUL KELLY GIG?) Still, the seed had been planted, and I like to think that as I matured, both as a person and a performer, the importance of things like kindness and compassion grew. This coincided with a burgeoning interest in spirituality, and whether you're reading yogic texts or a book written by the Dalai Lama, 'try not to be a cockhead' seems like a pretty universal ideal.

Friendship has always been important to me but so has connecting with people in my job. It's one of the reasons I so enjoy talking to my audiences. In fact, before I go onstage, as part of my little pep talk to myself, I often think about the crowd and about being as open to them as possible so we can really share the performance (as opposed to an actor friend of mine who when envisaging the audience before a show chants in his head, Fuck you, fuck you, fuck you . . .). I'd tried to expand on this with projects like the spirituality series, and not just because looking at bigger questions and involving others was a way of adding another dimension to my punchlines: more and more it was how I wanted to live.

One of the notions central to Buddhism is that a bird has two wings: wisdom and compassion. Equal emphasis is placed on self-knowledge and serving others. I liked the sound of this shit. And you know what? Altruism makes you feel good. I slowly recognised that I wanted to help others not just through what I do for a living but in any way I could. I felt that if all you can do with your privilege is feel guilty then you might as well just shoot another rhinoceros and invest in cryonics. Mind you, one day while I was grappling with this question, I saw a woman reply to a request to donate to an animal welfare group with, 'No thanks, I'm just an arsehole person,' so making a contribution is not for everyone. But the question for me was: what could I do with my extremely limited skill set?

I'd been trying to work this out for a while. After my most recent split with Mr Rabbit, it took some time before I even felt capable of turning my energy outwards, but I got a nice little kick up the backside following a grief-stricken therapy session.

I was picked up after the appointment by an Uber driven by Abeer, a Sudanese woman. I managed to choke out the words 'couple's counselling' while I hyperventilated in the back of her car. Abeer, sensing my embarrassment, proceeded to tell me the story of how her husband had left her. Despite the fact that she was now essentially a single mother there was not a shred of bitterness to her. Buddies had told her she should get on Tinder or start partying on the weekends so that she could meet someone new.

Instead she decided she'd rather spend her spare time driving for Uber and putting the money towards building classrooms in her mother's village. Abeer, a refugee, said that thanks to her grandmother she's a big believer in giving. Her feeling is that most people can offer *something* to help others; if you don't have money then maybe you have time. She was extremely matter-of-fact about it all.

This humble, extraordinary woman told me she enjoyed working for Uber in the main, but when she didn't, all she had to do was remind herself why she was doing it, and that was more than enough to motivate her. It certainly put my situation into perspective. When I managed to stop weeping, I told her my break-up story and she simply said, 'That's not depression, he's a thief.' There was no denying she had some good points.

We tracked Abeer down for the podcast, and more people have commented on her interview than on anything else in the series. She had no idea I was a comedian so was floored when she got the call from my producer, Karla. I don't know what surprised her more, learning that the hysterical mess in the back of her car actually earned a living from making people laugh or that my ride with her had meant so much. As she was leaving the studio, she gave me the green bangle she was wearing. She said it had brought her good luck and she wanted me to have it. I then asked if I could have the shirt off her back, her car and her eldest child. I took the bangle. I don't wear jewellery but I do wear that.

At the time I met Abeer I was still months off being much use to anybody but she at least got me thinking. The second little light-bulb moment happened at one of the few gigs I did in the months after the split, compering a benefit dinner for a local group called Space2b. This is an art and design social enterprise that supports newly arrived migrants, refugees and asylum seekers. I found myself sitting next to the main speaker for the event, human rights and refugee advocate, barrister Julian Burnside. At one point I said that I simply didn't know what to do about refugees and asked what he thought was the best way to help. His reply was, 'I don't know. I've tried everything I can think of. Your best bet is supporting local initiatives like this.'

It's embarrassing to admit but until that moment acting locally hadn't occurred to me. Ego was probably partly to blame for this. I had a profile, shouldn't I be saving *the world*? I hadn't had that actual thought, I'm not a sociopath, but it really hadn't entered my head that what was important was to do *something*, no matter how big, and that getting involved in my own area was a start.

Hey, it's not like I'd reached nearly fifty without ever trying to help others out from time to time. I'd volunteered at Meals on Wheels as a teenager and I'd done other stuff since then that involved more than just cutting up carrots. (I should probably mention that when I say 'volunteered', our school curriculum required us to either do some form of community service or attend a 'marriage' class. I was pretty confident that the latter would be an hour a week of people saying, 'Don't have sex yet,' which I already had covered, so I thought, Slicing root vegetables for geriatrics? Count me in.)

Years ago, I did some mentoring for a writing program connected to a magazine that published fiction by people living in halfway houses. I was placed with a grumpy, lean Englishman called Ed. The support was meant to last for six weeks but in the end our association lasted about eighteen months. I helped Ed put on a one-man show at La Mama, and it was extremely gratifying when I saw him some years later and he told me I'd helped him turn his life around. I know, I'm AMAZING. I don't think his comment is true at all: he was ready to change and I just happened to be there. I'd love to say that it had been a beautiful, heart-warming experience but in fact it was a time-consuming pain in the arse.

My annoyance had nothing to do with Ed himself, who's great (although I was resentful the night I took him to a poetry reading and someone thought he was my date – he's significantly older than me). It was just all so . . . inconvenient. I don't know what I'd been expecting, but I begrudged the time. I thought it was the right thing to do, to 'give back', but I'm equally sure I was doing it for selfish reasons, believing that the experience would make me feel wonderful and worthy, would fill a hole that my job couldn't and give me a warm sense of purpose. I may have grudgingly got the job done but it exposed me as an impatient, condescending wanker. That's not what I signed up for.

After establishing that one-on-one help was not quite for me and my very important life, I took up an offer to become an ambassador for ActionAid (finally, I had a title, although I would've been happier with baroness). ActionAid is an international charity with an emphasis on women's rights, now focusing particularly on communities affected by natural disasters. Not long after Mr Rabbit and I started going out, I went to Uganda with one of their Australian workers, Holly, and an Aussie photographer based in Africa, Miranda. We travelled with a local Action-Aid worker, a remarkable young woman, Kodili, and a driver, the only person remotely as old as me, Godfrey.

We were there for only ten days but it was extraordinary. You come back from somewhere like that and think, I can never complain about anything ever again. And then, of course, you do. We travelled all over the country and met people dealing with female genital mutilation, AIDS and incredible poverty. All of which compound the other rampant problems faced by Ugandan women – domestic violence, sexual assault and a lack of basic human rights. In certain areas, women have about as much freedom as cattle, and in some cases those animals are treated far better.

My job, or so I thought, was to visit various communities to see what ActionAid had accomplished while also learning what more needed to be done. This would be documented, and hopefully I would be in a position to raise awareness of the plight of these people on my return home. It turned out that my role was a lot more active than I'd bargained on. Of course, no one in Uganda had the slightest idea who I was, but they did know that I was an 'ambassador' and so mistakenly thought I worked for the government and was responsible for both past and future funding. I was expected to speak everywhere we went and was often greeted by songs, which I couldn't understand apart from the words 'Judith Lucy', before people tried to lift me up and carry me on their shoulders. No one who knows me is ever that pleased to see me.

I often felt like the Queen at these events, stiffly giving my thanks and telling them how the women of Australia would be so impressed by their accomplishments and would want to help them. I knew I was getting desperate when, at one village, I started quoting 'I am Woman' at them. What is it with me and that song? It's a tremendous anthem but telling a bunch of African women, in a language they couldn't understand, that I could 'hear them roar' must have made me sound like some insane white woman who thought she was on safari.

I met incredible people, though, and saw how little it took to empower those neighbourhoods. ActionAid had established vegetable patches on which the women could grow some of their food; they could then sell some to earn a little money. These positives were enough for their husbands to let them spend time outside the home. But what really changed these women's lives was meeting with each other and sharing their stories. They were no longer alone and suddenly had a tiny bit of independence.

Some of the problems these people faced were heartbreaking. I met a young boy with feet made out of wood, heard of a woman who'd had her back broken because she refused to sleep with her HIV-positive husband and met another whose genitals had been mutilated by her mother-in-law, who had first drugged her. Her husband left her shortly afterwards because she can no longer have sex and has difficulty urinating and defecating. She was now collecting honey, hoping to earn enough to give her three daughters more choices than she'd had so they'd escape the same fate. I'd never felt so white, guilty and useless.

When I went to Haiti with ActionAid several years later, not too long after my relationship ended, it wasn't quite as shocking as that first visit to a developing country but it was equally sobering. One of the reasons ActionAid focuses on places struck by disasters is that assaults on women increase dramatically in the wake of a hurricane or earthquake.

Who knew that while you were dealing with death, injury and lack of food and water you'd also feel like raping someone? It's clearly the only way some men can retain a degree of power. The fundamental issues are the same in Haiti as Australia, just much worse: the victims are blamed, what they were wearing is questioned, and the justice system repeatedly lets them down. In one story we were told, a preacher raped his housekeeper, who became pregnant and moved away; the preacher subsequently forced his daughter by the housekeeper to come and work for him when she was fourteen, raping her too. She also had his child.

I came back from both of those trips feeling lucky, guilt-ridden and filled with a desire to do more. ActionAid is a truly fantastic organisation, and I've tried to make the most of the opportunity they gave me by taking part in comedy nights for them and by speaking and writing about my experiences, things which are at least in my wheelhouse. I was always pretty scathing of actors and TV personalities campaigning for various charities until I became one myself. It's a tricky tightrope to walk: it's nice to be able to use whatever profile I have to help but I often feel like a well-intentioned, entitled mascot.

Once, I was talking about my trips on the ABC and the next day a woman came up to me in Coles and said, 'I heard you on the radio, aren't you doing some amazing things!' I replied, full of false modesty, 'Just trying not to be an arsehole,' and she then said, 'Keep working on that,' before disappearing down aisle five.

I may have made a little more progress than the woman who refused to donate to the animal charity, but I absolutely do need to keep working on it. I need to keep trying to educate myself about these women's lives or my empathy is really just pity. The inequity never stops making me feel uncomfortable, and it should. I remember how awkward I felt when I sheepishly raised the #MeToo movement with an incredibly impressive ActionAid worker in Haiti, Marie. The movement was at its height and I asked her how she felt about it, considering what the women of her country were dealing with. She paused before saying, 'We are all women, we need to hear your stories too.'

And I need to keep working on it for another reason as well: you can be an arsehole even with a cause. While I'd involved myself with ActionAid to advocate for these people, it was as much about helping myself. Worse, I had to admit that my attempts were more likely to happen when I was single. I just never felt the same urgency to make the world a better place when I had access to a penis.

The one exception to this was when I threw myself into the death-positive movement after my brother died. This attempt made particular sense to me because surely if we got better at dying we'd get better at living, and that could result in a whole range of positive changes for the planet, couldn't it?

The death-positive movement is sometimes referred to, hilariously, as death wellness – I'm not sure just how well you can be when you're, ahem, not living. The gist of it is that we've swept mortality and terminal illness under the funeral-industry carpet for too long. We've locked away the elderly and tried to avoid the pain and illness that often accompanies the dying process by taking it out of our homes and sanitising it as much as possible. It's as if, when it comes to the last part of our lives, we've all picked up a giant antibacterial-handwash dispenser hoping that if we slather on enough goop we can somehow avoid the messiness of our final act.

The first thing I attended was a death walker course. This is like becoming a midwife but at the other end of life, so fewer nappies and more shrouds. The role is to help the dying person and their loved ones deal with the last chapter. Death doulas, as walkers are also known, aren't just around for the big finish, but are an important part of planning for it and helping in the aftermath. On a practical level the course was enlightening: now I know what you can and can't do with a dead body. You actually don't need to involve the funeral industry at all in some states, and as long as you keep it cool, you can keep your corpse, *Weekend at Bernie's*-style, home for several days and then take it direct to the cemetery or crematorium yourself.

How I wish I'd known that anyone can be a funeral celebrant – I certainly would've done that for my brother. But would he have wanted us to keep his body in his bed as friends kept vigil? Would he have wanted us to bathe and dress him? Absolutely not. I don't think I'd want that either. I've gone out of my way to make sure most of my loved ones have never seen me undressed, and the thought of anyone having to deal with my naked quim is just repulsive. Of course, regrettably by that stage I'll know nothing about it, but the question is, would the sight of my lifeless vag be of help to those left behind?

I also learnt about green funerals, advanced-care plans, and even discovered that you can rent a coffin, but the most useful part of the course for me was hearing how men and women can deal very differently with dying. Mum had prepared for her own death, and when my friend Lynda Gibson was dying the whole affair was one of openness – she shared the journey with all of those lucky enough to have her in our lives. There were tears but also a lot of laughs, and Lynda made us feel comfortable by not denying what was to come. Men are apparently more likely to deal with grief by doing, not talking, and that went some way to helping me understand my brother's reticence when it came to discussing anything of much significance when he was dying.

Our death walker teacher, Zenith Virago (yes, she does live in Byron Bay), made the point that some people die just as they've lived, so if they've never been inclined to hold forth about their inner life, that's not going to change at the end. More comforting was hearing that just because someone isn't talking about what's happening to them, it doesn't mean they're not internally processing it. I so hope that my brother reached some sort of acceptance at the end of his life.

I started the course genuinely thinking I might become a death walker, but by the end my interest, if my notes are anything to go by, seems to have waned. I think I was just more interested in being part of the conversation about how to deal better with death, rather than being the person who helps you nut out a living will, or holds your hand as Grandpa takes his final breath. But I wasn't done with the topic itself.

Next I went to a death conference, which attracted everyone from academics to palliative care nurses to artists. Some of it was fascinating, like hearing about academic Pia Interlandi's dissolvable garments for the grave, but when I found myself dancing around a room wearing one black glove, singing, 'Let's Talk About Sex' with the word 'sex' replaced by 'death', I did wonder what the hell I was doing. The final straw was watching a woman stage her own death and funeral, complete with glowing eulogies. This was followed by an explanation that the participants were all just playing 'roles' that they were able to 'let go of' with some breath work. Having just seen all this happen to my brother for real, I found it to be one of the most self-indulgent pieces of bullshit I've ever had to sit through, and I used to be a drama student. Ultimately, I learned that the death movement is as full of whackjobs and wankers as any field.

Naturally, this seemed like fertile ground for the podcast. Something I hadn't yet done was actually spend time in a funeral home, where death is obviously a lot less theoretical. So I went to Natural Grace Funerals in Woodend, Victoria, which promotes a more holistic approach to dying, and was lucky enough to talk to one of the practitioners. She described recently watching a young man dig a grave for his father, one of the most moving things she'd ever seen.

I then watched in awe as a woman who'd been given six years to live planned her funeral while her four-year-old toddler played nearby. Her degenerative illness was already quite severe and by the end her quality of life would be all but gone, which was why she'd already started planning. Because of her condition, her speech was impaired and my producer and I barely exhaled while she was speaking – we didn't want to miss a word. It was one of the moments I was glad we were recording for a podcast rather than television, because a camera would have been too intrusive.

This remarkable woman doesn't believe in religion, wants to see the Northern Lights if she can get there, and is writing emails full of stories about herself and her children so that they can read them when she's gone. She wants Nirvana's 'Smells Like Teen Spirit' played at her burial – she doesn't want an actual funeral. She's taking care of all the arrangements so that her family and friends will have an easier time of it when she goes. To me it seemed then that her religion was kindness. She said all she wants at the end is peace.

Her husband wasn't up to joining her in this planning, and both she and the funeral director spoke compassionately about him and his inability to deal with the situation. I wasn't as sympathetic. For my money, it was just another example of the fairytale not living up to its publicity. Of course, I understand that what he's going through is horrendous too, but if marriage is 'til death do us part, shouldn't he be here supporting her through the process? Like many of her friends, he didn't want to talk about it because it was 'too morbid'. That denial was familiar. I sobbed when I got home that day because Niall wasn't able to do for his family what this woman was doing for hers. I cried for the people he left behind, but mainly I cried for him. And then I cried for me because I miss my big brother.

Most of the practitioners at the funeral home were female. Is it because we're returning to a time when death is a woman's domain again as it was before the industry became sanitised and monetised? Or is it simply because we've always been so much better at dealing with and talking about the difficult shit? We don't mind crying and being emotional. We don't mind the mess.

Something Zenith the death walker said, which I continue to think about, is that death is a way of touching the profound. She seems to be able to immerse herself in this world by embracing the mystery of it all. A lot of us don't have a church to go to anymore and I think that's why the popularity of the death-positive movement is growing. We're trying to know the unknowable. It's probably been obvious to you, but I finally worked out that's what I was really trying to do by throwing myself into this space. It was my way of grieving my brother's death and trying to make sense of my own. But it also confirmed that the best contribution I can make in this area is doing whatever I can to change the conversation.

I'd actually been talking about it in my work, one way or another, for years – a show I did when I turned forty ended with me getting the whole audience to chant, 'We're all going to die,' over and over as silver squares of confetti fell from the ceiling and I danced to the 'Tequila' song. Don't tell me that didn't change people's lives!

Six months after meeting Abeer, I became more involved in Space2b, which is just around the corner from me. I'd met the beautiful actor Clare Larman, a walking ray of sunshine, at the same dinner where I'd met Julian Burnside. She'd been volunteering with the organisation since the beginning and told me she was helping some in its community improve their English with conversation classes. This seemed like something I could do and we talked about possibly working together. A meeting with the founders of Space2b, Mariam and Janine, made us realise that what was needed even more than English classes was an evening to raise money and awareness. Clare and I thought we could put together a night involving comedy that people would hopefully pay to see (featuring me and Denise Scott), along with members of Space2b talking about their experiences of moving to a completely different country.

It was challenging. For starters, Clare and I simply had no idea how to go about it. I'm a comedian, she's an actor, but neither of us had ever put on a show with a diverse group of people whose first language wasn't English. The participants, almost all women, were from Nepal, Egypt, Chile, Somalia, India and elsewhere. Each had a remarkable story and most of them were harrowing. In one of the preparation exercises, we asked people what noises they'd been used to hearing when they woke up in their home countries, expecting replies like chickens or cooking. A woman from Afghanistan who wound up a refugee in Iran answered, 'Bombs.' Initially, she refused to tell her story onstage because she's Muslim and thought that even just seeing her hijab would make some people uncomfortable. Thankfully, she changed her mind.

The numbers ebbed and flowed – some people came to a few sessions and stopped while others came to one and never returned. In the end we had a core group of eight, but we really didn't know that until about two weeks out from the performance. We rehearsed in my local yoga studio, thanks to the generosity of my teacher, Louise. Clare and I very loosely organised the sessions around all sorts of questions. Anything from, 'What makes you laugh?' to 'What's a smell that reminds you of home?' The idea was simply to get people talking, which they did. When we heard a particularly powerful story, we would suggest that the teller write it down to perfect it for our evening.

I don't know who we were kidding. This is the sort of exercise you give drama students, not a group of time-poor people with no performing experience. So we jettisoned the idea of polished monologues (although I was still keen to do my Amanda Wingfield from *The Glass Menagerie*: 'That was the spring I had the craze for jonquils . . .') and let the evening evolve into something far more informal.

Many of the stories revolved around eating and the significance of sharing what you have with others. Women told of friendships that began over meals with neighbours or colleagues, but there were also too many examples of Australians turning their backs. So many times, Clare and I were embarrassed by how selfish and unwelcoming we can be in this country, even though we have so much. I don't think we understand how little it takes. One woman spoke of her joy when another parent at her child's school simply asked her over for a cup of tea.

Every session was full of both laughter and tears and the actual process was crazy – people had to juggle family and work, or looking for a job, with our little rehearsals. No one ever did the 'homework' we set because they didn't have time. That's why, in the end, the evening was more of a slide night with questions and answers. But everyone spoke eloquently and we ran way over time.

So much of putting the night together had been out of my control, and had put me out of my comfort zone again, but I didn't understand until later that this was actually the most valuable part of it for me personally, aside from the fundraising. It made me aware of my shortcomings and the areas I need to work on. When I first started reading about cultivating wisdom and compassion I think I took those two ideas to be separate. I didn't get that in trying to help others you can actually learn about yourself, and that's as significant as the good deed itself. I doubt I'll ever be at ease in these situations but dealing with that is one of the lessons I'll keep learning. Trying not to be an arsehole person turns out to be a lifelong practice.

I was happy that I was trying and I realised that Abeer was right: we all have something to give, it's just a matter of working out what part each of us can play in making the world a bit less crap. I was still feeling pretty lousy but at least I was busy, I'd moved on from spring-cleaning my flat to attempting to spring-clean my life. I wanted to clear out the old destructive habits and make way for the new! I was continuing to say yes to every invitation that came my way, from being involved in an art exhibition about writers to a sound-meditation evening at one of my local yoga studios.

I wasn't trying to numb myself anymore either because I now understood that my uncomfortable feelings weren't just about my personal fears, they were a consequence of living.

I'm pretty familiar with how grief works by now: you just have to go with it and there's never a time by which you 'should' be over it. You just feel terrible until you start having days when you don't. Gradually you get a few of those in a row, then a few more, and then one day you realise you haven't thought about your loss for a while and you surprise yourself. In my experience, it's usually at this point, just when you think you've turned a corner, that something pulls you right back into the abyss and the whole process starts again. We don't get over these heartaches. I can't see a day when I wake up and say, 'Thank goodness, I feel GREAT that Mum's dead now!' Instead, like the monkey lines around my mouth, they become a part of who we are.

11
Wouldn't be Dead for Quids
The Answer!

Who knew the podcast would actually come up with the answer? I had jokingly called the final episode 'Tying All This Crap Together', but it actually did!

I asked everyone who took part in the series the same four questions: Are you single? How do you feel about dying? What gives your life meaning? Are you currently overwhelmed by the state of the world? Looking back, I'm not entirely sure why I asked everyone if they were single. Possibly that was just a cry for help/thinly veiled pick-up line on my part. The answers to the other questions were wonderfully varied, with one of my favourite responses to the meaning question being *Judge Judy*.

Almost everyone was overwhelmed by the state of the world and the most common reason for that was climate change (this was pre that pesky pandemic!). This had slowly been making its way to the top of my list of concerns as well: I couldn't believe how long that'd taken.

I like nature. I mean, who doesn't? It seems to be something we all enjoy as children and despite my early love of watching television, I hadn't been immune to it. We'd had a great back garden with huge trees, flowerbeds that Dad had made and that Mum tended along with a thriving vegetable patch. There was also a huge pine forest across the road with all sorts of critters. Niall and I walked there often. I didn't understand it as a kid, because it was all I knew, but Perth is a little wilder than its counterparts in the east. The boundary between city and country is more porous and you're more likely to see an untamed animal in an unexpected place, such as the venomous brown snake that slithered into our living room. (At least I think that's what it was. I'm basing this on Mum's recollection and she was a little prone to exaggeration. It could have been a praying mantis or a tennis ball.)

Growing up – partly because I don't think Mum ever fell out of love with her homeland, Ireland, but also because of Australia's pervasive colonial hangover – my idea of nature was lush, green English countryside. I had little time for our native landscapes and flora – they were dry, drab and nowhere near as beautiful as the tamed gardens we saw on all the BBC dramas we watched. It made sense that I loved everything about Victoria when I first moved there. All that rain and verdant countryside were intoxicating and there weren't the constant blue skies and unrelenting light of my hometown. Melbourne was grey and urban and I could spend more time indoors being cultured and eating great food and drinking fine wine with no guilt! There were very few sunny days 'to waste' in this way.

I still love all that cultural side of Melbourne and I've never felt homesick but the appeal of grey skies and cold weather wore off quickly. It took longer for me to see that I missed the river and beaches of Perth. I might not have been a swimmer but I loved seeing so much water, which is probably why I still live in a bayside area. I miss eating outside and hanging out on people's verandas. Don't get me wrong, not enough to move back, but I didn't know how deeply ingrained all that stuff was.

Western Australia is in my bones. This dawned on me when I finally started reading Tim Winton. I'd resisted him for years simply because he was from Perth and had a ponytail. I'm not sure where that aversion came from. I don't generally judge people by their hair, with the exception of Donald Trump which I think is fair enough as he obviously says to his stylist every morning, 'Can you make my head look like a lyrebird's arse, please?' Then one birthday my very bossy birth mother bought me *Cloudstreet*, pressed it into my hands and said, 'I'm going to insist that you read this because I know you'll love it.' She knows me well. I devoured it and then read everything he'd ever written. I don't know any other non-Indigenous writer whose work quite captures how unique our country is, as well as how sacred. First Nations Peoples have obviously been across this for tens of thousands of years but most of the rest of us are only just starting to figure it out. We've been very good at thinking we're way more important than the land and we're certainly paying the price for that now.

I've been lucky enough to see quite a bit of this country, but it took a television gig to get me out into the Centre. One of the most remarkable experiences of my life came while filming *Judith Lucy's Spiritual Journey*. After a night in a hotel in Alice Springs we went camping just outside the town, under that endless star-filled sky, and spent time with three Aboriginal elders, Gloria McCormack, Maggie Cowins and Beryl Collins. The piece probably lasted about ten minutes on TV but we were there for a couple of days all up. My strongest memory, apart from what was captured on film, is of silence. It was a skeleton crew – just me, a producer, the director, one camera and sound person. There's always a lot of waiting around when you make television so you get used to making small talk. Not this time, though. We all found patches of shade to sit under while waiting for the right light or for someone to turn up or whatever it was, but we all sat on our own and barely spoke. It was hot, it was near the end of the shoot and we were tired from travelling, but that wasn't why we were quiet, and nor was the silence uncomfortable. I felt it was out of respect for the land and its custodians who were looking after us. We behaved as you would in a church.

It was the first time I'd really understood how inconsequential humans are and how much we need to respect what's under our feet. I was equally awestruck when I visited Uluru and Kakadu some time later on holiday with Jan. I was well into my thirties when I had these experiences and they led me to wonder how on earth I'd ever preferred trimmed green hedges and trained rose gardens over these marvels. I love this country. Every time I travel overseas it's confirmed: I wouldn't want to live anywhere else.

Climate change is a real downer, isn't it? It's not like I hadn't been aware of this; it was one of the reasons I'd stopped voting for the two major parties some time ago. I'd been doing all the things you're meant to: carrying my own little cloth bag, using more public transport, paying the carbon offset on plane trips. I recycled and ate less meat. In short, I tried to do the right thing without actually letting it affect my life too much because that enabled me to keep my head buried in the sand.

I didn't watch *An Inconvenient Truth* until quite recently for the simple reason that I knew I'd find it too depressing, and I hadn't done that much reading about it for a similar reason. I knew the broad brushstrokes: greenhouse gases, polar icecaps melting, species extinction, yada yada yada. I knew I wasn't doing enough but I couldn't engage because it was all so bleak. I'd also decided that this was someone else's fight. I was doing other stuff to try to be a good person – didn't Leonardo Di Caprio have this one covered?

But despite my spectacular gift for denial, it was getting harder and harder to ignore climate change, and then I realised that I'd shifted from trying to ignore it to being incapacitated by the enormity of it. Suddenly, the reason I wasn't doing more was I just didn't fucking know what to do. All I could see was how useless our politicians were, and how on a global level governments and big business were doing what I'd done – acting like it wasn't their problem. Even allowing for our eroded trust in institutions that are meant to be safeguarding our future, this seemed incomprehensible. Were we really putting short-term profits before the destruction of the whole planet? Yes, we were. What do you do as an individual when that's happening? 'Nothing' wasn't really working for me anymore so I decided to try the act-local approach again.

I live near the St Kilda Botanical Gardens and have a real affection for them. They're not big but they contain some of the contradictions of our country, with a native garden sharing the space with manicured flowerbeds and a fabricated lake. Standing in the lake is a sculpture of a little man holding an umbrella, and on a sunny day rain pours down on him from inside it, powered by a solar panel. The ducks keep him company, as do the players of the giant chess board nearby. There are always mothers and children in the playground and often people having a picnic, sunbaking or playing the guitar. The gardens are where community and nature collide, and what a fabulous marriage that is.

The park is also home to the Port Phillip EcoCentre, a community-managed environmental group. On one of the many days I spent beating myself up for my inaction on climate change and my lack of knowledge about sustainability,

I discovered I could volunteer at the centre. I was pretty vague about what I might be able to offer but it seemed like a step in the right direction, and was also not too many steps from where I lived. On my first day, I turned up feeling nervous, wondering at how, as a fifty-year-old, I could experience the same sensation I had in the schoolyard, when you feared that no one would play with you. I knew nothing about gardening, either, and had visions of accidentally digging up a rare species while my fellow volunteers looked on in horror and thought, Who is this moron?

The EcoCentre volunteers couldn't have been a friendlier bunch of people and I wasn't the only one who wasn't an expert on flora. Deb Punton, the coordinator, has the kind of enthusiasm that's just infectious – I found myself getting as excited about the worm farm as I would have if I'd really still been at primary school. Deb also made everyone feel competent performing the main tasks of weeding, planting seeds and pruning.

Tending the compost seemed to attract the few men who were volunteering. If I had to guess, I'd say that was because the task was always the same – cutting stuff up – so could be done with minimal interaction with others. And conversely, that was clearly why most of the women were there: as well as to help. These impressive ladies were retired and often donated their time at several places while sometimes also studying or writing. While the EcoCentre was one of many activities the women did, I came to feel that for the men it was more like a lifeline.

There were also a couple of younger volunteers, and I was told their numbers are on the increase. Who wouldn't want to be outside among living creatures in these gorgeous gardens? Friends couldn't believe that I'd started gardening but I can honestly say that having my gloved hands in the dirt made me feel better than I can tell you. It still does. Watching things grow is neat. What could be better for the soul than digging around in the soil while chatting to like-minded people? Lunch, that's what. After gardening for about three hours you eat a delicious meal, also made by volunteers, with the produce sourced from the garden. It's a truly wonderful way to spend a Friday morning.

It's made me want to have my own garden. My hope is that when I can finally buy somewhere to live, I'll be able to have a patch of green I can cultivate. I never used to understand the appeal but now I know why people find gardening so relaxing and rewarding. Is it just getting older? Do you turn fifty and suddenly rediscover some of the wonder you experienced as a child? Or is it the realisation that bulbs are fun and won't give you a three-day hangover?

The EcoCentre also houses the Bay Keepers, who collect plastic waste from around St Kilda Beach and document it. I asked Deb if this was depressing and she said, 'Yes but you immediately feel better by doing something.' This attitude would become another theme of the podcast series. In fact, for the first episode we interviewed the author of *The Happiness Project*, Gretchen Rubin, who agreed with

Deb that the best antidote for anxiety is action. Deb also introduced me to a grassroots organisation called Climate for Change that brings people together to discuss climate issues, their impact and the actions that can be taken. We taped one of their evenings for the show and it reminded me of a sex-toy party (I mean, I've read about them), just with more talk of flooding and droughts and fewer dildos for sale. Deb played a movie on climate change, which we all discussed along with what measures we'd already taken in our lives and what we hoped to do in the future. This was all done over a wonderful homemade vegetarian soup and a glass or two of wine, and it gave us the opportunity to connect with people of all ages about our frustrations, and our despair.

There seems to be an idea that climate change is a cause largely taken up by the young, but that hasn't been my experience. It certainly wasn't that evening, or when a group of elderly women, complete with placards, stood outside my local train station for weeks demanding action on this issue. It didn't seem to be prompted by anything in particular; it was as if a bunch of older Balaclava ladies just woke up one morning and said, 'Right we've had it. Fuck the knitting, let's protest!' I'm heartened by this because it's everyone's problem.

At the other end of the spectrum, one eighteen-year-old broke all our hearts at the Climate for Change gathering when he told us that he'd just got his driver's licence but was trying to use his car as little as possible for the sake of the environment. I know this all sounds rather comfortable and easy, and that we don't actually have the time for another glass of red and a civilised chat about the state of the world, but the older I get, the more I think that this is how movements coalesce and tipping points happen. We all need to do much, much more but I also believe that all the little things add up.

Deb also runs Tune into Nature workshops. Having dealt with her own grief and paralysis over climate change, she's interested in connecting people to the natural world as a form of healing and inspiration. I heard Richard Powers talk about something similar in an interview. His latest novel, *The Overstory*, is about trees and I couldn't put it down. I'm not going to try to describe it but I urge you to read it. What I will say is that I see trees differently since reading this book. More accurately, I really *see* trees for the first time. When I'm in a train or a car, they are what my eyes seek out now. I'm one of many who's had that reaction to the novel and Powers talked about how, when we feel that we're a part of the natural world, we can't help but want to preserve it.

My own Tune into Nature experience with Deb was like going on a date with a shrub. First she got me to choose a tree I felt drawn to in the gardens. Then she encouraged me to engage with it – I touched its bark and crushed and smelt its leaves, but not before asking its consent. That's correct, I talked to a plant. Yes, it does sound like I'd lost my mind but I found just being present with this living thing truly moving. At one point I couldn't stop smiling but then I thought I was going to burst into tears. I was overwhelmed by the life of this tree and all it supported both above and below ground. I'd not long finished *The Overstory* and had had very little sleep, so I'm actually surprised I didn't propose. That's an option I'm still considering. It would be even better than committing to a guy in prison. Not only would I always know where my husband was, but a tree would be less likely to stab me!

Among many other pieces of wisdom, Deb said something that I've come to believe: how can we ever be lonely when we're surrounded by all these living creatures? Which in turn reminded me of something Indigenous writer and performer Steven Oliver said when we interviewed him for the podcast: 'I think Mother Earth is the ultimate church.' Steven told the story of an uncle alone out on Country who talked about being 'surrounded by all this family'. This was echoed by Tim Winton, who said, 'One of the things that has given my life meaning is realising that I'm in a relationship with the natural world.' I spent so many years desperate for a root. Turns out it was for a root of a very different kind.

This was all terrific but walking down the aisle with a tree didn't seem like the ending to the podcast series I was looking for, and I also didn't know where we would have got my pulpy partner a suit.

I don't ever really expect an enterprise like a TV show or podcast to contain a life-changing revelation. Not if I'm at the helm anyway. I talk to people who invariably know a lot more than me about most things and hope they'll give the audience a takeaway. *Overwhelmed and Dying* had covered a lot of ground. The glue was still me trying to discover how I could make the most of the time I have left on the planet, and as you've seen, the themes that emerged were the importance of connection and community, countering anxiety with action, and the pull to being a part of something bigger in light of life's uncertainty. All of this was on my mind when I was trying to think of an ending.

I thought it might make sense to finish at some natural wonder of Australia, like the Great Barrier Reef, and after a weekend down the rabbit hole looking at possibilities, I eventually hit upon Ningaloo in Western Australia. Not only is it one of the last remaining healthy reefs in the world, but twenty years ago it was saved from development by a grassroots campaign, and so was testament to what people can accomplish when they band together. I also knew that a new campaign was under way to stop a multinational, Subsea 7, building a pipeline assembly and launch facility in the nursery of the reef, Exmouth Gulf.

I knew all this because Tim Winton had written about his involvement in the battle to save Ningaloo, both the initial one and the current one, and I hoped that the reef might 'tie all the crap together', especially if we could get an interview with publicity-shy Winton. I'd also read that swimming with the humpback whales and whale sharks is a life-changing experience. And by some miracle, all the pieces fell into place – my producer Karla and I were off to WA!

The schedule was tight for those few days in my home state. We started by recording a piece about my brother at one of his favourite drinking haunts in Fremantle, Little Creatures. His ashes are scattered nearby at South Mole because the place meant a lot to him and his family. Niall and I had gone there together not long before he died. We actually used to visit as kids with Dad, to get saltwater for his fish tank – a waking nightmare. Getting the water was precarious, but nowhere near as challenging as dealing with our mother when we got home and walked half the Indian Ocean through the living room to the tank, which was generally home to rocks and dead fish. Good on my brother for making some new memories for himself. He's made them for me too. I don't think about our parents arguing anymore when I go to South Mole, I think about Niall.

I dropped in on Mum and Dad too, at the site where their ashes are buried in Karrakatta Cemetery. I'd never visited the place before. People had assured me that seeing the plaques would be deeply moving. Karla and I spent two hours wandering around the enormous graveyard and we never found them. I'm now fairly convinced that they faked their own deaths and are living the high life in Buenos Aires. Good luck to them, I hope they're happy. To be completely honest, I think we hoped that the visit might add some emotional heft to the final episode, so that plan really went to shit. That's the problem with any sort of documentary-making: reality doesn't always play ball with your storyline, and we didn't know what we'd get out of our trip to Ningaloo.

The next morning, after having spent a night gorging ourselves on homemade fish pie at Jan's, we caught a plane to Learmonth Airport. Tim picked us up and immediately took us out to the red canyons of Cape Range, where we interviewed him. I make that sound like it was something I did most weekends, but the truth is, I WAS BESIDE MYSELF.

I'd actually met Tim before. I first interviewed him during my breakfast radio days. Thankfully, we weren't in the same studio (he was in Melbourne and I was in Sydney), so he couldn't see how nervous I was. We made small talk while an Anastasia track was playing and I'll never forget him saying he liked my voice. I know that a lot of people don't so that was a pleasant surprise, but when he went on to say it reminded him of one of his primary school teachers, a woman 'we were all scared of but I think we all had a crush on her too', I nearly burst into tears. Admittedly that happened a lot when I was working for Austereo but the chat with Tim almost made that awful year worthwhile.

It was certainly one of the very few times when a celebrity lived up to my admiration of them. (Lenny Kravitz also didn't disappoint; let's just say that when Kaz Cooke and I talked to him for our weekend radio show, there wasn't a dry gusset in the house.) I met Mr Winton in the flesh a couple of times after that and even hosted a Q&A with him about his book *The Shepherd's Hut* for the Melbourne Writers Festival. Every time I meet him, I'm struck by his humility and how considered he is. I couldn't have cared less about interviewing Brad Pitt (which I also did for the radio) but when Tim is around, I behave a bit like a teenager meeting a member of their favourite K-pop band.

Tim talked passionately about the campaigns past and present, along with how places like Ningaloo give us all hope, and how swimming with whale sharks makes you realise that we're all just 'cosmic dandruff'. So that's what we set out to do.

Early the following day, Tim, Karla and I went out in orca specialist John Totterdell's boat to explore the reef. I already knew that this part of Western Australia was stunning and I was excited about what was in store, but I never could've predicted the effect this trip would have on me. I was in such a state of euphoria that I managed to ignore my terror of putting my head underwater. Here's my tip: if your lack of a basic skill might endanger your life, just ignore it! (And maybe take a bunch of experts with you.)

First, we saw humpback whales breaching. I'd never been so close to one of those sublime mammals. It's impossible to describe the feeling of awe at being up close to a wild creature in its natural habitat. IRL really is the best, isn't it? In the same way that you can't compare a live performance to a recorded one (yes, it is a little sad that this is my frame of reference but it's all I've got), having water sprayed in my face by this bus-sized animal crashing into the ocean right in front of me turned my grey matter into confetti. Soon we were in the water, snorkelling with manta rays, those bizarre, graceful bats of the sea, and I couldn't stop wondering how I had wound up here. Me, a city slicker who could barely swim. I don't think I need to add that I was way out of my comfort zone yet again, but the difference was that I didn't have time to notice because I was just too full of wonder.

Close to the end of the day, John told us to jump into the ocean once more, *now*. A minute later I was gazing down at what I presumed was the seabed, wondering what we were about to see. Suddenly I realised that I was already seeing it: about eight metres below us hung a whale and her calf, their scale so huge I could feel what was left of my confetti brain struggling to adjust. It literally took my breath away. In fact I was so discombobulated that I did actually stop breathing and started kind of drowning. That's not an exaggeration, I forgot how to function. My whole life, I've been way too much in my head but for once I wasn't thinking anything. I was just *completely there*. Turns out meditation has nothing on the thought-stopping awe of the natural world.

I had a repeat experience a few weeks later when I went back to film a story about the new campaign to save Ningaloo for the TV show *The Project*, and went out with Tim and John again. By a minor miracle, we found a whale shark, completely out of season. Again I was speechless. If anything this was even more astounding, because we had more swimming time with it and I was actually remembering to breathe. Also the whale shark was at eye level, so I could really take in the sheer scale and beauty of it.

Tim had mentioned that the experience of snorkelling with whales never loses its magic and I don't see how it could. There was another bonus on top of all of this: due to my lack of competence in the water, Tim had to hold my hand the whole time. Bummer.

When I got back into the boat after each of these experiences, I was simply overcome. I had to sit down and I felt like bursting into tears. The centre of our country had made me understand how insignificant humans are, but that amazing red dirt couldn't look me in the eye the way that whale shark did. I did indeed feel tiny enough to be washed away by some cosmic Selsun Blue. All our obsessions, from wrinkles to mortgage repayments, just seem completely ridiculous when you're confronted by something that size alive in the ocean. You get a glimpse into the history of this planet and everything that inhabited it before we came along with our petty desires and laughable ideas that we could ever really tame or control any part of it. Why would we even want to? I hadn't expected snorkelling with these giants to move me so profoundly, or to energise me as it did: I want to act in whatever way I possibly can to preserve that place. Tim had already said it in our interview and he was right – everyone should have the opportunity to have this experience and feel this sense of reverence, or at least know that it's a possibility. It's simply beyond my comprehension that we would jeopardise that for some short-term gains for the oil and gas industry, especially when we've already compromised so much of the planet for them.

I just felt like an idiot. Why hadn't I seen the crux of the matter before? I care about a lot of issues but none of them will matter if we're trying to live on a giant ball of fire. What could be more precious than the earth and all the creatures who share it with us? How much longer are we going to keep trashing it? I don't know if it's too late or not, but as one of the founders of the good-news email, 'Future Crunch', Tane Hunter, said when we interviewed him, 'If the world ends, I want to be at the party where we all sit around saying that at least we did everything we could, as opposed to the one where pessimists sit around saying, "I told you so."' I know which party I'd rather be at too.

I'll never forget those two dives at Ningaloo. When I was about to jump into the ocean the first time, Tim had said, 'Did you think you'd be doing this in your fifties?' Well no, Mr Winton, I did not. Life can be relentless and difficult but sometimes it's just plain fucking wonderful. I never would've believed that at fifty-one I'd be swimming above a humpback whale with Tim Winton holding my hand, and if that's not a reason to get up in the morning I don't know what is. I feel like I've spent so much of my life searching for a purpose, for a feeling of belonging to something greater than me, without realising that I was already in it. I was already here. When I said to Tim, 'Wouldn't be dead for quids,' he replied, 'Couldn't even arrange it.'

12

There is No Answer

Wouldn't that have been a beautiful ending? I had found my answers: nature, action on climate change and connection. I was in touch with my body and fine with being single. I was still on the journey but that was going to be part of my powerful and wise conclusion, because isn't it all a journey, people? I was over my ex and ready for the next chapter of my life. I was still dealing with menopause but was planning to come off HRT and embrace my inner (still bewitching, still sexy) crone. I'd thought about shit and thought about it and I had dealt with it! NAMASTE EVERYONE! HELLO LIFE! THE BEST IS YET TO COME!

Then the pandemic hit.

I think I speak for quite a few people when I say that COVID-19 COULD NOT HAVE MADE ME FEEL

MORE SINGLE. The pandemic revealed that my idea of being happy on my own was built on very shaky ground.

The joy of living alone is very much predicated on the notion that you can choose to see people whenever you like, and with that ability taken away, it suddenly seemed unbearable. I cannot imagine the challenges faced by people who were locked down in share houses or in situations that were toxic or even dangerous. I was safe from those things in my nice flat and I had work. I know I was one of the lucky ones but it was *lonely*. In Victoria, you were permitted to see a lover but not a friend. My buddy Andrea, who also lives on her own, wanted to come over for a cup of tea but I said, 'Hey, to keep this legal you're going to have to sit on my face.' Apart from anything else, this would have made it tricky to drink my Earl Grey.

The word that kept circling my brain during lockdown, as I know it did for many, was 'should'. I should be working more, I should be helping people and I should be using this time constructively. I should not be drinking this much. I should not have stolen toilet paper from the airport, and I should be not just coping but thriving! This should be a time of reading, reflection and inquiry that confirms some of my recent realisations and builds on them.

Fuck that. I did keep up my yoga practice but mainly I drank, got stoned, watched TV, did the minimum amount of work possible and generally marinated in a pool of self-hatred. In other words, I went back to all my old habits, but this time they didn't make me feel safe.

THERE IS NO ANSWER

Mother's Day fell while we were all in our home prisons and I rang Jan as usual. This always feels like a weird little betrayal of Ann. I heard how Jan and her sister and my cousins were all together for lunch outside. I love this family but I'll never be a part of it in the same way I was part of the one that raised me. This sort of thinking might explain why, when unexpectedly confronted with the possibility of discovering who my birth father was during lockdown, I was ambivalent.

At the start of 2020 on the verge of writing this book, I checked Ancestry.com again, hoping an intriguing relative might have turned up to swell my word count. The website tells you which of its customers are DNA matches with you and can pinpoint how close the relationship is. A second cousin, who isn't related to Jan, had recently joined and emailed me. This was the first time the website had turned up someone who might lead to my birth father. Not all families want to let the skeletons out of the closet, so when I explained that I was hoping to find my dad I didn't know how she'd react, but she was enthusiastic about making a project of me and spent the next few months trying to figure it out.

Initially, my friends seemed more excited than I was, but I think my reticence was a defence against disappointment. I'd spent years reassuring myself that I was fine with not knowing who my father was, and now I didn't want to set myself up for a fall. My newfound cousin began her research and sent me photos of relations of hers who might have been my birth dad.

After a few red herrings, towards the end of April, I sent Jan a picture of a young dentist and she heard the ding of a distant bell. Their connection had been brief and time had blurred the details – in Jan's recollection he'd been a chemist – but this possibility seemed worth exploring, especially because she still found the young man in his dental outfit attractive. I should mention that he's dead; he died of cancer thirteen years earlier. People who heard this were sad for me but because I'd never known anything about him, I considered everything a bonus. If he did turn out to be Dad, I'd also have three half-brothers, which seemed like a good result.

My cousin was extremely well intentioned but I baulked when she said that I was now part of their family. I'll always be grateful that Jan is in my life but our reunion was not without its complications and that was difficult to explain to my new relative, who now had a pretty interesting tale to tell at dinner parties. Understandably, the family were confused by my reticence. It took weeks before I rang the dentist's widow to see how she felt about one of her children taking a DNA test, but she was warm and supportive. Again, I took my time contacting her son who'd offered to take the test. It wasn't just because I wanted to take my time with the whole process, I was also flat out doubting every part of my life again.

This round of self-questioning was different from the last – it contained all the old favourites but with new angles! Refreshingly, I wasn't doubting my career anymore, quite the opposite; no one was more surprised than me, but the prospect of never performing in front of an audience again genuinely upset me. As I write this, theatres in Melbourne are starting to reopen and it will be a slow road back. It only took a pandemic to make me realise that there really is no business like show business and I love being a part of it, especially when I'm not actually doing it. Thank Christ I'd finally stopped wondering whether it was too late to become a blacksmith.

The real revelation was that my stress levels during lockdown were pretty close to how I felt MOST OF THE TIME. What had I been doing? I needed an income but I hadn't been driven by the need for recognition for years and I'm not really big on owning stuff, so why had I spent so many hours fretting? No one was holding a gun to my head to force me to work as hard I did. I wanted a house and some security so that the next time the phone stopped ringing I wouldn't have to panic, but I WRITE JOKES FOR A LIVING. If I crack a bad one someone will probably think about it for less than a second before they go back to thinking about their own shortcomings. I didn't have to be a doctor to work out the effects adrenaline and cortisol had taken on my body over the years, along with all the self-medicating I'd done. Jesus Christ, how many painfully obvious revelations can a chick in her fifties have? Yes, I'd definitely been trying to shut out general feelings of uneasiness about living and life but now I finally understood that a lot of me numbing myself was so I could just get by. Keep going. When I locked the door it wasn't only about trying to feel secure, it was about having a break from stress for a few hours so that I could get up the next day and do it all again. Many times I'd thought that I should stop doing so much of whatever it was to deaden my emotions, but the most obvious solution hadn't occurred to me: I needed to start living differently. I needed to give myself a break.

I think I'd always equated looking after yourself with self-indulgence. Maybe I'd taken my cue from Dad again, who, when he had a massive heart attack, refused to let my mother call the doctor and instead spent the day doing someone's tax return while in excruciating pain. Finally, Ann ignored him and called an ambulance. Did I need it to get to that point? ('I don't care if my face isn't moving, doctor, I really need to finish this punchline!') Holy hell, did I think a bit of self-care was weak? I'm only just starting to understand that being a little kinder to yourself (which in my case involves decisions like: don't go out with fuckwits, don't let yourself be treated like shit and don't give your money away) also means judging yourself much less harshly.

I think a lot of us grew up without ever understanding the concept of self-love or self-compassion, or we confused it with narcissism. A common insult in the playground was 'You love yourself.' Imagine if I'd said, 'Well, yes I do actually and so should you.' A nun probably would have given me a good thrashing.

I didn't properly understand that other people's feelings towards you, like so much of life, are changeable, and

THERE IS NO ANSWER

largely beyond your control. I know now that relying on anything outside of yourself for worth is never going to pan out well.

I finally understood that the person I had to commit to was me.

No, I'm not about to marry myself, but it's a continuation of what I discovered about looking after my physical needs; it's about investing time in my own life by making plans that involve only me. Ann Lucy's generation grew up with the motto 'others first, self last' but if you constantly ignore your own needs, caring for others just isn't sustainable.

I'm not saying you can sort yourself out by buying a book on self-compassion, lighting a ylang-ylang candle and having a nap, but I am saying, especially if you're a woman, you're worth more than most of us have been led to believe, and you deserve to find your North Star.

Another revelation for me was that this stuff takes work and discipline. I've never been short on that when it came to my job but it had never occurred to me to put that kind of effort into my wellbeing. You have to actively choose to spend more quality time on yourself, as opposed to quick stress fixes. You have to work at changing the thought patterns that have constantly reinforced that you deserve less; you have to start making decisions that make you feel worthwhile. And those are going to look different for every woman.

Maybe you need to tell your partner you're not going to be the one who deals with his family anymore. Maybe you need to start booking yourself holidays or getting the kids to wash their own clothes. Maybe you need to pursue that passion you put on the backburner because you've been too busy looking after everyone else's needs. For me, it's giving myself permission to enjoy the work I do but also acknowledging that I'm more than my career, and not every part of my life has to wind up as material. (I will stop doing that as soon as this book goes to the printer!)

It's about giving up on the crazy notion that everything I do has to be perfect. It's taking some time off, it's saving money for my future, it's looking after my health better, and really working at silencing the negative voice in my head that tells me the only time I'm worth it is when I buy a L'Oréal product.

A line I've used more times than I care to admit is 'I don't know anything about anything.' Like most of us, when I was younger I thought I knew it all. Life is constantly forcing us to let go of everything, including our assumptions and our sense of self. Every time I think my ego can't take another hit, it does, and should. Sometimes that's been brought on by suddenly understanding a motivation, like my need for male affirmation, and occasionally by hanging out with a giant fish. And just when I think I've figured stuff out there'll be a pandemic to deal with. Or I'll think, Okay, fine, I know what works for me, here's something I can rely on. And then that will be taken away or stop working, whether it's my latest HRT medication or a drink.

What I've actually finally realised is that all this is what growing up looks like. It's not about learning to do my

THERE IS NO ANSWER

tax (thank Christ, because that's never going to happen) or buying a house or having a family or a partner. I kept waiting for some version of all this to happen, not understanding that it wouldn't make me an adult. You need to accept that you'll keep fucking up again and again and there are absolutely *no* guarantees. No matter how hard you try to secure things, the rug will always get pulled out from under you. All you can do is get better at standing up again once you've fallen over.

Towards the end of writing this book both my shoulders went on me, which made it excruciating to type and impossible to do yoga, the one thing I'd come to depend on to keep me sane. There was that damn rug-pull again, but it didn't stop me thinking, Are you fucking kidding me? Does this shit ever end? It reminded me of one of my favourite scenes from the very camp *Damages* when Glenn Close's character, at her hammy best, whispers and then shouts, 'I get it, I get it, I *get it!*' There's never anything to hold onto. It never ends. I GET IT.

Wait.

I know, it's getting a little ludicrous, but I really did think that was going to be the end of the book because I'd always wanted to combine Buddhist philosophy with the lead actor from the movie *Albert Nobbs*.

Like I said, there's always more to the story and there's now a new chapter to mine. On 18 June 2020, it was confirmed.

The dead dentist is my father.

I have three half-brothers.

I'd done my best to mentally distance myself from the outcome of the DNA test and yet when I received an email from one of my (I can now say) siblings confirming it all, I was genuinely delighted. He and I and another brother Zoomed two days later. I don't think it's hit any of us properly and I've no idea how involved we'll be in each other's lives, but I like them. I learned that my father was a decent man and that means a lot to me.

Nothing is ever simple, though – his widow is adamant that I'm a cousin, not a half-sibling, because sibling-only tests are never a hundred per cent conclusive. But the chance that my half-brother and I share a parent is 91.4 per cent and that, combined with Jan's memory, is good enough for me. I was conceived a couple of years before my dentist father met his wife. I'm trying not to take her stance personally, and she might not always feel this way.

So a question I never thought would be answered has been. None of us knows what will happen when we meet in person. Nor will this be the end; families have a habit of constantly remaking themselves.

What a journey for my other, very decent birth parent too. Jan sent me an email saying, 'Dear Judith, Thinking about you. I am so glad that now we know who your father was. But am so sorry that he is dead and that I have had to put you through all this. Lots of love Jan.'

That's not how I feel at all and I told her so. I don't have any feelings of anger about anything Jan did, only grief that the family I grew up in is gone. But that doesn't mean that there's an end to how I feel about the Lucy family. Not long ago, I came upon a letter Dad had written to Mum, presumably just before he died. It reads in part: 'I want you to know that I love you as always and to thank you for sharing so little.' (Presumably he's referring to not being enough of a provider.) 'The only horror of "shuffling off" would be in my neglect to communicate my feelings to you and to let you know how much I appreciate you being my wife. Who knows, I may still get the chance to prove it but if I don't I'll have to settle for my intentions and a bitter disappointment.'

So in the end, Mum did know that she was loved by Dad. When she was ill and at her least attractive, he constantly told her, and us kids, how much he adored her. I'll never know what triggered this change in his behaviour – I suspect a combination of age and guilt about his past treatment of his wife. It didn't matter. It made Mum happy. But I feel that the rest of us shared, to a degree, Dad's 'bitter disappointment', because we just couldn't seem to make our little family work. Inherited pain and confining roles destined us to conflict and misunderstandings, but we did all love each other. Even Niall once loved Dad, before damaging notions of masculinity brought their relationship undone.

I'm still angry at the men in my family but I know that will fade. I needed to view them through a critical lens to try to make sense of some of my own actions and beliefs, but I'm aware that in so doing there's been little room to explore their narratives. I'm not done, though. Their memories live with me and will keep changing and forming new connections.

Pieces of them are in my nephew Dylan too. Sometimes when I walk beside him and see him from the corner of my eye, Dylan could be my big brother. I love this sweet young man without end. Jan wondered how Niall would have dealt with me having three half-brothers. I know the answer to that question: very badly. And yet, as when I met Jan, it wouldn't have and never will affect my feelings for him, or any of them. Twenty years after their deaths, my parents still loom very large in my life, as does my brother six years on. I remain a Lucy.

And I remain a part of Jan too. I have an image of her to which I often return: she is stepping out of a cloud of drizzle at a cousin's outdoor wedding, walking towards me with arms outstretched, saying, 'Isn't this exciting?' I'm lucky to have this curious, positive, warm woman in my life. I just wish that in some parallel universe she could've had some of my childhood and Mum some of her freedom, but both women were restricted by the times they were born into.

Despite the limitations of her life, I see now that Mum was a seeker. She tried so many different things and when she experimented with yoga and Transcendental Meditation, she was way ahead of the pack. Like my brother and father, though, I never took any of this seriously. I undervalued almost everything about her, including the fact that she was a mother. I dismissed one of the most amazing aspects of being a woman. I don't know that it would have made me feel differently about having children, but I wish I'd taken the time to even consider it. I wish I hadn't, for so long, seen my body as an inconvenience instead of a thing of wonder. I certainly no longer deny how important Mum's religion and faith were to her. Something in me yearns for what she craved too. If she'd lived, I don't doubt that she would've kept exploring life and been one of those women who volunteer their time and energy for what they believe in.

I am now one of these women. I have another single lady as my emergency contact. I may join a book club or take up bridge. I'm not going to buy a cat but I want to garden, cook more, ride my bike and walk in nature. I even took swimming lessons last year so I can hopefully hang out with a whale again someday.

I want to keep searching and learning and letting go until the very end.

Acknowledgements

Thank you to everyone at Simon & Schuster especially Dan Ruffino, Michelle Swainson, Barney Sullivan, the very patient and helpful Meredith Rose, and Jo Lyons for her suggestions. I guess I should also thank that Ben Ball guy who I followed to Simon & Schuster. I would follow you anywhere Ben.

I'd also like to thank everyone at Token Artists especially Kevin Whyte, Dioni Andis and the live production team particularly Kath McCarthy, Rowan Smith and Nathan Pettenon for all their work on *Judith Lucy versus Men*.

Thank you to the ABC for letting me make the podcast series *Judith Lucy: Overwhelmed & Dying*. A big thank you to my excellent Executive Producer Tom Wright and my equally excellent Producer Karla Arnall.

I'd also like to thank everyone who was involved

in the making of that show: Brendan O'Neill, Abeer Elamin, Gretchen Rubin, Jan and Alice from Icebergers, Shae Graham, Dr Jen Martin, Dana Parker, Vanessa Muradian, Greg Taylor, Nikki Britton, Dean Arcuri, Brett Blake, David Leser, Prue Spencer, Nicola Gidley and Lee Cohen, Glenda Lehmann, the members of the Space2b community: Anu Bajwa, Tadros Ibrahim, Sharife Amiri, Pamela Mujica, Sumaya Yusef, Lhakpa Lobsang, Maria Alejandra Valenzuela, Muhubo Sulieman and co-founder Janine Lawrie, Rebecca McCabe, Tane Hunter, Climate for Change, Robina Courtin, Libby Maloney, the incredible anonymous woman who let us be there when she planned her funeral, Stephen Oliver, Tim Winton, Denise Winton and John Totterdell.

Thank you also to my friends who were involved in the series: Ash Flanders, Jayne Dullard, Andrea Powell (and thanks to your much-loved mum Nola), Stephen Briggs, Gareth Skinner, Denise Scott and Kaz Cooke (thanks also Foxy for your invaluable contribution to the cover and the manuscript and for being my cheer leader when I wanted to stop writing and become a beekeeper).

Thanks also to Zenith Virago and Michelle Temminghoff from Passionfruit who were not in the podcast but were definitely part of the journey.

Thanks to Jan Healy, Dylan Bray-Lucy, Colin Batrouney, Deb Punton, Clare Larman and Garrity Hill for reading parts of the book and not wanting to kill me.

ACKNOWLEDGEMENTS

I'm also going to thank some friends who haven't been mentioned yet because you contributed to the book and/or simply because you had to listen to me bang on and on and on about this motherfucker: Holly Miller, Julia Holmes, Daniel Hugh Manning, Annie Maver, Robyn Byron, Warwick Hunter, Andrew Creagh, Sue Bignell, Justine McDermott, Jo Chichester, Anne, Michelle, Michael and Mark Hovane.

Thank you to all my families: the one I was adopted by, the two families that my birth parents are a part of and the family that I've made for myself.

About the Author

Judith Lucy is the bestselling author of *The Lucy Family Alphabet* (winner of an ABIA for best biography) and *Drink, Smoke, Pass Out*. She also happens to have performed numerous one-woman shows (most recently the acclaimed *Judith Lucy versus Men*) and the recent smash hit *Disappointments*, with good friend Denise Scott; won numerous awards (including the 2017 Melbourne Comedy Festival's People's Choice Award); created two ABC TV series (*Judith Lucy's Spiritual Journey* and *Judith Lucy is All Woman*) and one ABC podcast (*Overwhelmed & Dying*); and swum with whales.